CONTENTS

The author, Alonzo Baker, and his sister Alma on her
ninetieth birthday.

My Sister Alma and I

By Alonzo Baker, Ph. D.

Pacific Press Publishing Association
Mountain View, California
Oshawa, Ontario

Design by Cliff Rusch
Cover photo by Persuasive Productions

Library of Congress Cataloging in Publication Data

Baker, Alonzo Lafayette, 1894-
    My sister Alma and I.

    1. McKibbin Alma Estelle Baker, 1871-1974 2. Baker,
Alonzo Lafayette, 1894-   3. Seventh-Day Adventists—
United States—Biography. 4. Teachers—United States—
Biography. 5. College teachers—United States—Biography
I. Title.
BX6193.M25B34   286.73[B]   80-16754
ISBN 0-8163-0373-8

Off to a New Start in Life

My sister Alma, the eldest child in the family of Stella and Alonzo Lafayette Baker, came into this world on a farm in Webster County, Iowa, in 1871. Soon after little Alma's birth, Father Baker, who had become more and more disillusioned by farming, decided to leave the farm. When Baby Alma was but six months old, Father announced to his wife that he intended to take the family and go West. He had relatives in Sonoma County in California. There they would visit, and perhaps they would make their home in California.

Mother Baker packed the things they would take with them after Father sold the farm and most of their possessions. The family left Iowa for the West. Upon their arrival in Sonoma County, Mother exclaimed over the beauty of the place. "Never in my wildest dreams," Stella Baker said, "have I imagined such beauty!"

But an even greater surprise came when Father located his relatives in a small town just west of Santa Rosa and found that they, who had been strong Methodists, were now involved in a strange new religion—Seventh-day Adventism.

At that time J. N. Loughborough and D. T. Bordeau, two young Adventist preachers, were holding evangelistic meetings in Santa Rosa. Father's relatives told him they had been attending the meetings regularly.

5

Now they invited Alonzo and Stella to attend also.

"I wouldn't go across the street to hear any preacher preach," Father sneered. He had been in the Union Army during the Civil War, and while on sentry duty he had read a book written by Tom Paine and another by Robert Ingersoll, both writers rampant and avowed atheists. Although Father Baker had been reared an orthodox Methodist, after reading those two books he had become very skeptical and atheistic in his own views.

But Mother Baker attended several of the meetings and felt impressed that what she heard was the truth. The more she talked to Father about what she had heard, the more disturbed he became. At last he told his relatives and his wife that he would allow her to hear no more from those crazy Advent preachers. And emphatically he added, "We are leaving California tomorrow!"

Father had read in a San Francisco newspaper that gold had been discovered in the Rockies just west of the San Luis Valley in Colorado. He proposed to take his wife and little daughter, now a toddler, there. Never again did he want to hear the name Adventist.

However, Mother Baker did not forget the truths that she had heard proclaimed in California. Even though miles away from her husband's Adventist relatives and although she had not become a baptized member of the Seventh-day Adventist Church, she studied and prayed and lived up to all she knew to be truth, howbeit her husband did everything he could to dissuade her.

Having heard about a weekly Adventist Church paper published in Battle Creek, Michigan, Mother Baker decided to subscribe to it. Not a single copy did she ever receive, for Father intercepted the mail at the town's tiny post office. He brought the papers home, but while standing over the wood-burning stove in the kitchen, he tore them up and dropped them into the fire. "Here goes your blankety-blank Advent sheet into the fire. Watch it burn!" he sneered.

As little Alma grew older, she felt the constant pressure in the home. When arguments erupted, as they often did, little Alma would run away to some hiding spot and cry until she could cry no longer. She loved both Mother and Father dearly. If only she could please both of them and avert the angry words and dissensions that arose between them.

When she could be with her gentle mother, sitting on a footstool at Mother's feet listening to her read stories from the Bible and explaining Bible truths, these were the happiest moments of her childhood. At an early age she learned to know and love her heavenly Father. Throughout her life she eagerly anticipated His second coming.

Father often called little Alma to his side in the evenings and told her over and over, "When you are grown up, you will be a teacher. You will go to school soon and learn all you can so that you can teach others."

Alma could not understand what Father was talking about, for the family was quite isolated. She had no idea what a school or a teacher would be like. She was seven before the family moved to a place where there was a country school. Alma's father told her she would at last be attending school. She must learn all she could, he insisted. She must obey the teacher in everything. Father also told her that should she be punished in school she would also be punished at home.

With lagging steps the little girl said good-bye to Mother and Father and the younger sister who had been born in Colorado, and started off to school. Never had she seen so many children running and shouting at play. When the bell rang, Alma followed the children into the schoolroom. From nine in the morning until four in the afternoon, with one hour free for lunch, Alma sat at a desk much too high for her. All she had to do was print words on her slate. The hours dragged. How she looked forward to the noon break and to going home after school.

During the lunch break one day, Alma sat on a swing,

her feet making the swing go back and forth.

"Let me push you high," one of the big girls offered. The girl began to push Alma on the swing. Higher and higher the swing went.

Alma trembled with fear as the girl pushed her higher. She couldn't speak, for her throat seemed to constrict. Suddenly she felt herself falling. She landed on the ground with a thud. The frightened teacher and some of the older students took the badly hurt child home. It was some time before Alma recovered from that fall. Then she came down with whooping cough. Her first school year had to come to a sudden end. And before the next school year began, the family moved. Alma would now attend a large ungraded school. The teacher had piercing dark eyes. Alma felt terrified of him. He seated her at a table, and on a stool much too high for her. "You are the only beginner in the room so you better learn in a hurry," he remarked.

But Alma, terrified of the teacher, seemed incapable of learning. It wasn't long until the teacher had dubbed her Dunce!

One day he sent a note and a list of words home with Alma. The note requested her parents to teach her to spell the list of words she had taken home, "if they could." They did. Alma could spell every word on the list that night before she went to bed. But, alas, when the teacher asked her to spell the words for him the next day, her mind went blank. The letters simply would not come. The teacher's patience gave out entirely.

Soon after that experience Alma came to school with a severe cold. She felt utterly miserable and could not recite her lessons. The teacher raged, "You are a dunce indeed. The slowest child I have ever known. If you can't recite your lessons tomorrow, you'll have to wear a dunce cap and stand in the corner all day."

Alma staggered home from school that evening with a high fever. Immediately Mother put her to bed. When the doctor came, he diagnosed her illness as being pneumonia with symptoms of brain fever.

8

For days Alma moaned and tossed in her delirium. From time to time she cried out, "Dunce! Dunce!"

During Alma's illness Mother gave birth to another child, the third girl in the family. When Alma recovered sufficiently from her illness, she fell in love with the new baby. She wanted to be with the little one constantly. She rocked the baby in the cradle, she held the little one's bottle, she even tried to wash the baby's clothes. With a new baby in the house, Alma felt secure. She would never have to go to school again, for surely she would be needed to care for the little one!

Happy School Days

One day Grandma, who was staying with the Bakers, remarked that soon Alma should be going back to school. At that the child burst out sobbing. It took some time to get her to tell her mother and grandmother why she did not want to go back to school. At last the story came out.

Grandmother straightened up, and her dark eyes flashed. "Well, I never! I'm glad that teacher is gone," she exclaimed.

"Gone! Where did he go?" Alma asked, drying her tears.

"We don't know or care." Grandma patted Alma's head as she looked down at her tear-stained face. "He was sent away while you were sick. There's a lovely young lady teaching at the school now. You'll like her," Grandma promised.

Alma wished she could feel as confident as Grandma. Teachers were teachers so far as she was concerned. She couldn't imagine one that would be kind—kind like Mamma or Grandma.

All too soon the day came. Alma hestitatingly trudged off to school. Although the sun shone warmly and meadowlarks trilled and warbled from fence posts beside the road, Alma felt, heard, and saw none of these. When she entered the school yard, she shivered. If only she could run away and hide. The last of the line of children had just entered the schoolroom as Alma came to the steps of the schoolhouse. She froze as she looked up to see the open door and the teacher standing there.

"I wonder if this is little Alma who has been so ill." The teacher smiled and spoke softly.

Alma nodded.

"I'm glad you got well so you could come to school while I'm here." The teacher took Alma's hand and led her into the schoolroom. "There, let me help you take off your wraps," she offered, stooping down to help the child unfasten her cape.

Alma stood still and gazed at her teacher. Words wouldn't come. But she knew she would love this teacher all the rest of her life. If she were to be a teacher as father wanted her to be, she wanted to be just like this teacher.

Miss Gould, the teacher, led her to her own big desk and brought a chair. "Here, Alma, I would like you to sit by my desk. Now, I see you have your primer with you. Show me how far you have read in the book."

"I—I—" Alma began and looked down at the floor. "I'm still on the first page because—because I—I can't learn to—to read. You see, I—I'm a dunce." A crimson flush crept over her face and neck. Tears came to her eyes.

The teacher put her arms around the little girl. "Who said you were a dunce?"

"Mr. Goff said so," she spoke almost in a whisper. "He was going to make a dunce cap for me." Alma looked furtively around as if expecting to see it somewhere in the room.

The teacher looked into Alma's eyes. "Mr. Goff made a mistake. You are not a dunce. I can tell by your bright eyes. They are just as bright as any in this room." Then she turned to the other children and spoke in a clear voice so all could hear, "Pupils, aren't Alma's eyes as bright as yours?"

Alma hardly dared to look at her classmates, but she

did look around from under lowered head and eyelids. Every hand went up. Some put both hands up.

"There," said Miss Gould, "everyone knows you aren't a dunce. You can learn to read. I know you can."

From that day on Miss Gould praised everything Alma did in school. She insisted that no one ever learned so quickly as Alma did.

With Miss Gould's praise and encouragement Alma had very little trouble getting through her primer. However, she never tried to read anything on her own until one Sunday when Grandfather brought home a Sunday School paper.

Alma took the paper from him and looked at the pictures. There was a picture of Jesus on the cross. Under the picture were lines of poetry. Alma looked at the picture and then at the words beneath the picture. Suddenly the words took on meaning. She read:

> There is a green hill far away
>> Without a city wall,
> Where the dear Lord was crucified,
>> Who died to save us all.

Over and over she read the lines. She had read them without any help. She *could* read. Now she began on the front page of the Sunday School paper and read every word in the whole paper. Thrilled with her accomplishment, Alma began to read the newspaper.

"Mamma," she called when she came to a word she couldn't make out, "what does r-e-n-d-e-z-v-o-u-s spell?"

"It's a French word and means a meeting place," Mother said, pronouncing the word for her. "But, child, why do you ask? I thought you couldn't read."

"I couldn't until today. I just learned how to read by myself. Now I'm reading in the newspaper about some bandits in northern Colorado. They have a rendezvous near Boulder."

The look of surprise and happiness that Alma saw on Mother's face made her more determined than ever to learn everything she could learn. Reading became so important that many times she had to be reminded and even reprimanded for not attending to other duties.

Children in those days were graded according to the reader in which they were studying. Alma soon could read any of the readers in the school. It seemed that her hunger for learning could not be appeased. Alma spent long hours at the globe in the schoolroom endeavoring to find countries about which she had been reading. She wanted to learn all she could about this great, wonderful world.

Never had the Bakers had contact with Seventh-day Adventists after returning from California. But Mother Baker never gave up the faith she had learned about in Sonoma County. Father still did not think much of her religious convictions, but he had ceased to harass her. Now Mother subscribed to the *Review, The Youth's Instructor*, and the *Good Health* magazine. Since Alma had become an avid reader, she read these magazines from cover to cover. From these papers she learned the names of all the Adventist workers and knew where they labored. She thought of Seventh-day Adventists as "Mother's people," and she hoped to meet and know some someday. Having read about Sabbath School, she wished she could attend. But there seemed no chance at that time.

Just before entering her teens Alma went to live with her grandparents in a small town. There were better educational facilities in the town, and Alma had gone as far as she could go in the ungraded country school she had been attending.

Alma found things much different in this town school. All her classmates seemed very interested in their personal appearance and their dress. Because she had a chubby freckled face and wore no bangs as was the style at that time, the students called her Fatty or Freckles.

Although she smiled and tried to appear nonchalant, the teasing bothered her. One day she decided to do something at least about her freckles. For three nights in a row she applied to her face some lotion she had been given called "Lily White." On the third night she awoke in great pain. She could not open her eyes. Her face seemed swollen to twice its size. Painfully she struggled out of bed and felt her way to the washbasin. After filling the basin with cold water and wetting a washcloth in it, she held the cloth to her throbbing and burning eyelids. But the dreadful pain continued.

Alma, still holding the cloth to her face, heard the door open and someone come into the room. As she turned to see who had come in, tears streamed from her swollen red eyes.

"I heard you stirring around, child, and I came to see what was the matter. Oh, Alma, whatever has happened?" Grandma looked alarmed as she stared at Alma's swollen face.

Between sobs Alma poured out the story. Grandma went to work immediately to do what she could to relieve the pain. She heated water and applied fomentations to Alma's face. That relieved the pain somewhat, and for two weeks Grandma continued the treatment.

When Father and Mother Baker came to town to visit and saw their daughter's swollen face as she lay in bed in a darkened room, Alma's mother exclaimed, "My poor child! She is blind! She will never see again." She began to sob.

"Am I blind? Will I never see again?" The thought almost overwhelmed the child.

"Is it true, Grandma?" she asked when her parents had hurried from the room. "Is it true? Am I blind?"

Grandma sat down beside Alma and put her arms around her. "Now, calm yourself, child. We hope the infection is only in your eyelids, and it has not impaired your vision. Let's wait until the inflammation is gone and you can open your eyes before we come to a conclusion."

Then she added, "My dear girl, I wish you had told me how you felt about your freckles. I know it is hard to listen to people calling you names and ridiculing you;

14

but everyone has some defect, some blemish. In the beginning God gave man a perfect body, but because of sin no one is perfect now. But when Jesus comes, we shall have perfect bodies and shall be very beautiful in face and form.

"There is a work for each of us to do. There is a special place for you to work, my dear child, and your success in that work does not depend upon your face or form but upon what is in your heart and mind."

Alma sighed a deep sigh. She resolved never again to worry about her freckles. "If I can see again, I will always try to help others and I'll find the place of service in life that God wants me to fill," she promised.

After two weeks in bed in a darkened room and after having regular treatments with hot fomentation cloths to her swollen face, Alma found one day that she could lift one eyelid a little. She also discovered that by sitting up, lifting the one eyelid, and looking down she could dimly see the pattern in the rug on the floor. Soon she could open both eyes. She saw Grandma standing by the bed. Then at last she could read a book. With the realization that she could see clearly again, Alma determined that she would guard everything she looked at from then on. She would look at only those things that were good and true.

Conforming to the World

Soon after the experience with the freckle cream, Alma's parents moved into town, and Alma went home to stay with them. Since there was no Adventist church in the town, Mrs. Baker decided to attend the Baptist Church, the only church in town.

"We are not giving up our faith," Mother Baker explained to the children. "We are Sabbath keepers and always will be. But since there is no Adventist church nearer than Denver, we'll attend the Baptist Church for now."

The Baptist Church had only eight members, but the services were well attended. Nearly all the children in town attended the Sunday School. Father Baker seemed happy with this arrangement. He had no objections to his family's attending any church so long as it was not the church of those "crazy Advents."

Alma, the light of his life, he still hoped would become a teacher. Since she had become such an avid reader, he subscribed to the *Youth's Companion,* a secular magazine, for her. The stories and articles taught high ideals in morals, education, temperance, and patriotism. It also contained biographies of famous personalities.

After reading a few issues, teenage Alma became fired with zeal for the temperance cause. She wrote an essay on temperance, but no one ever profited by it, for she felt too shy to deliver it at her school. However, she did slip into the barn and deliver the message to the family cow.

My sister Alma seemed to be always thinking of others and what she could do to help them. Near the Baker home lived a poor woman, Mrs. Slover, the mother of three young children, who took in washing and did ironing for people in the town. Each day on her way to and from school Alma passed the small house. Often she stopped to talk to the woman and play a few moments with the children. Alma's heart was touched many times as she saw the poor woman bent over her washtub scrubbing clothes on a washboard or wearily pushing the iron that she heated on her cookstove back and forth over the clothes that she then had to fold and deliver.

One winter the youngest child came down with pneumonia. The mother looked even more tired now. Alma knew she nursed the child through the nights and still washed and ironed during the day.

One Saturday evening Alma had accepted an invitation to a party at a classmate's home. Not being much interested in parties, Alma had not planned to go, until her father insisted.

On her way to the party she passed the home of the Slovers. Then she decided to retrace her steps and find out if the sick child were improving. Alma noticed that the mother had dark circles under her eyes and that she staggered as she walked. The little one lay in his crib unconscious and breathing heavily. All at once the party seemed of no importance at all. Here she could do something to help.

"Show me how to care for little Henry," she said to the tired mother. "I'll take good care of him while you lie down and rest."

"Oh, could you for just an hour or two?" the mother asked. "Wake me in a couple hours." The weary mother sighed as she took off her shoes and lay down on the bed in an opposite corner of the room. Alma covered her with a blanket, and almost immediately the woman fell asleep.

Alma attended to the baby. Then after stoking the fire in the kitchen stove she sat near the baby's bed. What would her father say when he learned she had not attended the party? she wondered. But then she reasoned, "He often sits up with sick folk; and if he knew how tired Mrs. Slover is, he would certainly want me to relieve her."

The clock on the shelf ticked away the hours. Alma sat up all night, watching the little one, doing what she could for him, and then dozing between times.

At dawn Mrs. Slover awoke. "Oh, my dear child, look at the time. It is morning already. I am so sorry I slept so long. Why didn't you waken me?" She hurried over to look at her child. The little fellow opened his blue eyes and looked up at his mother. A smile formed on his lips as she bent over him.

"Thank God," the mother exclaimed. "He's going to be all right."

Alma felt well paid for her evening as she hurried home to meet her family.

Father Baker met her as she came in the door. "Where have you been?" he demanded.

"Oh, I stayed at the Slover place all night. Mrs. Slover needed to rest. Little Henry has been so sick, you know, and she has been up night and day."

"Well, do you mean to say you sat up with a sick baby all night instead of going to a party? That's not normal for a child your age." He shook his head but said no more.

Father did all he could to persuade Alma and her sisters to conform to the world and be like their classmates. On the other hand Mother Baker tried to instill in their young lives a love for Jesus. She taught them to be true to what they believed. She taught them the commandments and the truth of the three angels' messages. As Alma grew older, she had to decide many times between the two ways of life. It was hard to form friendships with those who did not have the same principles that she held dear. She did not dance or attend the public skating rink as did her classmates. She dressed plainly because Mother insisted Adventists were plain people. They did not follow the extreme fashions of the day and wear hoops and bustles.

"Why don't you dress like the rest of us?" the girls at school asked. Alma knew they giggled behind her back because she wore only a gathered skirt on a plain bodice instead of the hoops and bustles. But finally they decided that she was hopelessly different and it was no use trying to change her.

During her first year of high school the English teacher assigned each student a composition. Alma had the topic "The History of Our Town." Early and late she worked gathering material of early days from old settlers. On the Friday afternoon when the compositions were to be read in school, the editor of the town paper came. He highly praised Alma's paper. Mother whispered to her after the editor had congratulated her, "Someday you will write for our Adventist papers."

The barrier between Alma and her classmates continued to grow. As time went by, her sense of isolation became a cross almost too heavy to bear. With the coming of summer came the greatest event of the year—the Fourth of July celebration. There would be a parade in which every soldier had a place. There would be patriotic speeches, a picnic dinner, fireworks, and—to climax everything—a grand ball.

Alma decided she would attend the celebration with the others of her school.

A new white dress hung in Alma's closet. Father had bought it for her as well as a white hat trimmed with blue flowers. Father had also bought a bracelet for her. These things he had given her when he had seen her high grades at the end of the school year.

Little twinges of conscience pricked her when she picked out the hat with the blue flowers on it. She knew that Adventists did not wear artificial flowers, feathers, or jewelry—and there was the bracelet. But just this once she would look like the other girls. Instead of the fashionable hoop and bustle, she starched a ruffled underskirt until it stood out stiffly.

On the morning of the Fourth, Alma dressed early and slipped away from home to join the other young people. That day her classmates greeted her warmly, and they accepted her into their circle. It being a warm day, soon everyone began to talk about going to the drugstore for a soda. Fred, a leader in the group, invited Alma to accompany him.

Although she had never acquired a taste for soda water, Alma decided that if this was a part of being accepted, she would drink it if it choked her.

Somehow the taste of that soda gagged her. She simply couldn't drink it. But to cover up her failure to enjoy the drink, she began to relate anecdotes about different people. Everyone laughed at her stories, and Alma felt elated at her success.

"Are you going to the grand ball at the town hall tonight?" Fred asked.

Alma ignored the question. But when Fred asked her to go with him to the play before the ball, given by members of the Baptist Church, Alma willingly agreed.

After the play Fred, who seemed to have become quite enamored by her, asked her to accompany him to the ball.

"I—I—think I'd better go home," Alma said. "I don't dance. It would be no fun for you."

Fred walked home with her, assuring her that he would teach her to dance. Before saying good night he told her that he had enjoyed being with her, that he had had a lot of fun. She waited just inside the door while he walked down the steps and went back to the ball.

Then with a heaviness in her heart she went up to her room. Suddenly every foolish thing she had said and done that day came to her mind vividly. She felt sick at heart. She took off her flowered hat and tossed it on her bed. Her bracelet she dropped on the floor, and it rolled under the bed. After undressing and putting on her robe, she walked over to the window and looked out into the darkness.

She could have friends if she would give up her ideals and plans that someday she would be one of "Mother's people." Tears filled her eyes, and she wept. Then kneeling by the window, she poured out her heart: "Dear Lord, I can't hold out any longer by myself. Please send an Adventist to our town to help us. And, dear Lord, forgive me all my foolishness."

A calmness seemed to come over her. She got up from her knees and slipped into bed. Almost immediately she fell asleep.

Two weeks later two Adventist ministers from Denver knocked on the Bakers' door. They had brought a tent with them and had come to hold a series of meetings in the town. Alma felt that the coming of these men was a direct answer to her prayer. She attended every meeting and drank in every word. How she thrilled to hear the truths presented one after another! The plan of salvation opened to her mind as never before, and she accepted it.

But a struggle began. The evil one said, "You have gone too far. Your sins are too great. You can't be forgiven."

Despair swept over her. She suffered agonies of remorse and regret. Was she lost? She told no one of the struggle, and she kept on attending the meetings. Then one Sabbath day the minister talked about the treasure hid in the field. How Alma longed for that treasure! Nothing else seemed important to her. If only she could be freed from her guilt and have the treasure. She stayed for the testimony meeting at the end of the service.

"These people are happy. They have never sinned as I have. I am unworthy to sit with them," she thought as she got up and went to the back of the tent. There she knelt down all by herself and wept with a broken heart. "O take my sins away," she pleaded.

Then a wondrous thing occurred. A glorious light shone upon her, and a voice said, "I forgive you all your sins."

Immediately the sense of guilt left her, and an indescribable joy filled her whole being. She rose up exclaiming, "My sins are all taken away. Jesus has saved me!"

What a time of rejoicing followed! The ministers and all the people, especially Mother Baker, knew that Alma had won a great victory and had been truly converted.

When the tent meetings ended, only Mother Baker, Alma, and her grandmother were ready to be baptized. Others had begun to keep the Sabbath, and they were studying further before baptism.

Before leaving the little group, the ministers organized a Sabbath School which met in the Bakers' living room. Alma was appointed Sabbath School superintendent and teacher of the children's class. At last she could attend a Sabbath School. How she had longed for that!

The year of her baptism was also her senior year of high school. She had the honor of being valedictorian of her class, and her speech was titled "Never Too Old to Learn." Her great desire now was to be permitted to continue her education and go on to college. One sentence in her speech seemed to sum up her desire. "Though the hairs of our heads become as white as the snow on the peaks that surround our mountain home, we shall never be too old to learn new things nor to share them with others." Surely the way would open for her to go on in her attainments.

A Dream Realized

Mother talked about a college in California, at Healdsburg—a Seventh-day Adventist college. She even sent for a catalog. But Father did not share her interest. He voiced his opinion that there was no reason why Alma should not now begin to teach. After all, that had been his desire all through the years of her schooling. She had received acceptance to take the teacher's examination. But God had other plans for her, and He worked a miracle—two, in fact.

Father Baker, now dealing in real estate, had sold a large ranch and received a good commission. One of the Adventist ministers and Mother Baker urged Father Baker to send Alma to college.

Much to Alma's amazement and joy he finally not only consented to send her to college at Healdsburg, California, but to take her there himself and see her enrolled and settled in the students' home. Now Alma certainly believed more fully the text that said, "All things work together for good to them that love God, to them who are the called according to his purpose."

Before leaving her at Healdsburg, Father paid up her tuition for two years saying, "I may not be able to do this for your sisters. If I can't, I shall expect you to help them."

The college admitted only devout and consecrated men and women, for it was a school for the training of

23

workers for the cause of God. Most of the students were old enough to know what they wanted to be and do. Alma, the youngest in the dormitory, had often prayed for just one girl friend of like faith! Now here she was surrounded by many. These friendships became true and lasting and a help in developing her Christian character.

Judged by modern standards, the school was a very simple institution. Its curriculum, limited to the essentials of knowledge, was taught with great thoroughness. No one questioned the quality of its teaching, for it had great teachers, and the teacher is the school. The enrollment never reached beyond 250 students in any one year. To avoid debt the school operated as economically as possible.

W. C. Grainger held the office of business manager, bookkeeper, and dean as well as being the president. He had no secretary. He also acted as first elder of the church—and a father to everyone.

Alma often marveled how one man could always be ready to help a student with a Latin translation, prove a theorem in trigonometry, or set one right on a biblical chronology then turn about and teach an inexperienced girl like herself how to develop a Sabbath School lesson so that she could teach it successfully.

From the first day of school until the last, Professor Grainger impressed every student with the importance of the Sabbath School. He called it the practice school of the normal, or elementary education department. He often commented, "Here you will learn how to teach the Bible to all ages. Begin with the children and advance until you can teach adults." It was an unwritten rule at Healdsburg that no one should refuse any task assigned him or her in the Sabbath School. The students were assured that help would be provided according to their need.

Therefore, when Alma was asked to be the assistant secretary not long after coming to the school, she accepted. Every Tuesday night she attended the teachers' meeting at the church. A record of the attendance had to be kept by the assistant secretary. Seldom did a teacher absent himslef. A written excuse had to be presented for each absence, and after the third absence that person was dropped and another one chosen to teach. During the first half of the teachers' meeting the leader gave instruction in methods of teaching. Then the teachers separated by divisions, and the leader in each division taught the lesson to a group of teachers.

Alma's ability as a teacher and a leader was soon discovered. Under the direction of Mrs. Caldwell in the primary division, Alma learned a great deal and found joy and satisfaction in her work. She looked forward to each Sabbath day, when she would have about fifty boys and girls and nine teachers before her for one whole hour.

All too soon the second school year at Healdsburg came to an end. The tuition that Alma's father had paid when she first came had been used up. But her course of study would take another year. She wrote her father asking if she might stay one more year and finish her normal training.

When the reply to her letter arrived, she eagerly tore open the envelope and read: "I cannot afford the expense of your staying on for another year. I am sure you have had enough education now. You can come home and teach in the public school."

Leave the school? Leave her friends? Alma felt crushed. There was still no Adventist church in her hometown. She would have no association there with young people of like faith.

Slowly Alma put the letter back in the envelope. Then she went to talk to her friend Clara Coney. When Clara, the Sabbath School secretary for the conference, needed assistance in her work—particularly the secretarial part—she often used Alma's help. Now Alma told Clara her problem. She would have to return home and teach in a public school.

"But, Alma," Clara interrupted her. "I've a plan.

Let's help each other. You know I've been wanting to go back to school and take some advanced Bible. With all the work I have to do, that's impossible unless I have help. So here's my plan. If you will help me with my secretarial work, I'll divide my salary with you. Then we can both attend school. How about it?''

Alma's eyes shone. "Clara, do you mean it? Could we do it?''

"Of course. Now let's talk it over with Professor Grainger.''

The girls found the professor in his office, and they laid their plans before him.

"A splendid idea.'' Professor Grainger approved. "It will help you both.'' Then turning to Alma he made a suggestion: "I think it would be good experience for you to spend the summer vacation at the Bible Training School in Oakland.'' At the school and under the supervision of Miss Burrus, later a missionary in India, Alma learned many valuable lessons in soul winning. However, during the last six weeks of training, each student was required to spend part of each day in the colporteur work. With no instruction in the art of salesmanship, Alma started out in her territory in Berkeley, California.

The weather had become unbearably hot that summer in Berkeley. Several died of the heat in the city. Alma had sold only two books during her days in the field; and she felt hot, tired, and discouraged. Upon starting down some steep steps from a house where there had been no one at home, she tripped and fell to the bottom of the steps. Overcome by heat and fatigue, she could not get up but crawled to a faucet near the porch. There she was able to reach up enough to turn on the faucet and let the cool water drip on her head. She lay in that spot until sundown, when she managed to stagger to the streetcar and get back to the training school.

For two weeks she lay sick in bed, suffering from heatstroke. From that time on Alma had to take special precautions and keep her head covered when out in the sunshine.

Fortunately when school started in the fall, Alma had recovered from the heatstroke and she enrolled in classes. She planned to finish her elementary education training that year and to learn the work of the Sabbath School department thoroughly under Clara Coney's direction. The two young women roomed together, and because they had so much office work to do, they were given the largest room in the dormitory.

That year Alma had the task of corresponding with persons who were conducting Sabbath Schools for isolated people. She encouraged these leaders and suggested plans and devices for their work. She also helped to establish the kindergarten division of the Sabbath School Department. But a pain in the back of her neck soon developed and became more and more severe. Although she tried to ignore it and put her self unreservedly into her work and her classes, the pain persisted.

When Clara, her roommate, came down with pneumonia that December, Alma nursed her back to health and also kept up with the office work; but the pain in her neck had spread now along the entire length of her spine. She slept little and soon could not digest her food.

Then one day in chemistry class one of her classmates held a lighted match near the tank where she had been collecting gas in a glass jar. A violent explosion followed. Broken glass cut her hands and face, and she herself was thrown against the wall.

That day, January 14, 1892, was the last day Alma ever entered the classroom as a student.

Although she felt better on Sabbath, and on Sunday morning got up to write a letter to a mother of five children who found it difficult to conduct Sabbath School and make the lessons interesting, Alma began to feel violently ill. She staggered to her bed and fell on it in a convulsion.

When the doctor came and examined her, he reported to her roommate and the Graingers that she would not live till morning. In her delirium and convulsions she could not be left alone. Mrs. Grainger and a nurse stayed with her through the night, one on either side of the bed to keep her from falling out.

"My Grace Is Sufficient"

The doctor had said Alma would not live through the night. But Clara Coney called all the girls in the dormitory together in the parlor while Professor Grainger and the other teachers met in his office. They earnestly prayed that Alma's life would be spared.

Morning came; and although weak and suffering intensely, Alma began to toss and turn as she thought of her unfinished work. She did not recollect what had happened in the chemistry class, but she thought of a letter she had been writing a few days before. She had not finished writing it. If she had gone right upstairs to the room after worship that morning and not taken extra time in the worship room, the letter would have been finished, she thought. She cried out, begging for forgiveness for her thoughtless delay. Then a heavenly being seemed to be standing beside her. He had a beautiful white robe over his arm, which he wrapped around her. At once she knew this robe was Christ's righteousness. All at once the meaning of righteousness by faith became clear to her. A great peace came over her. The pain in her spine eased, and she slept.

"Where are all the students?" Alma asked when she awoke. "Why do they not get up and go to school?"

"Why, it is in the middle of the morning. They went to classes two hours ago," the nurse told her.

For two weeks the girls dressed quietly each morning

29

so as not to awaken Alma. They tiptoed down stairs in their stocking feet and put their shoes on only when they were outside the dormitory.

Professor Grainger wrote to Mr. and Mrs. Baker, telling them of Alma's illness. Mr. Baker answered by return mail: "I took a perfectly well girl to you. If she is sick, it is because of the way you Adventists live. So take care of her."

Certainly the dormitory was not the best place for a sick girl. One day Professor and Mrs. Grainger came over to Alma's room. They wrapped her in blankets, and Professor Grainger tenderly carried her across the lawn to his home. They had set up a bed in the sitting room, and there Alma lay until the end of the school year. Mrs. Grainger cared for her as if Alma were her own daughter.

Every time Alma tried to move about, convulsions seized her. A great fear came over her that she would never be well again. At last she mustered up enough courage to ask the doctor.

For a moment he did not answer. Then he spoke quietly. "It is a long lane that has no turn, and if I do not see a turn in your lane, it is not positive proof that there is none."

The meaning of the doctor's words weighed heavily on the girl. Now what could she do? The Graingers had planned to spend the summer in the High Sierras with their son who was not well. Certainly if she remained at their home, they could not go. What could she do? She didn't want to be a burden. There was but one recourse.

Calling Professor Grainger to her bedside, she asked him to make arrangements for her to go to the poorhouse.

"Why, Alma, I could not put my little sick daughter in the poorhouse," he replied. "There must be some other way. Give me a few days to think about it."

During Alma's years at Healdsburg she had met a young man, Edwin McKibbin, who had been teaching in the preparatory department, the secondary school.

Alma and Edwin had become more than friends. Edwin had before this asked her to become his wife, but she had felt a responsibility to help her sisters with their education. The young man had smiled and said he would wait.

Now that she was so ill and the doctor gave little hope of her lasting more than a year, Edwin McKibbin insisted that he should marry her and take care of her as long as she would live. He talked it over with Professor Grainger and the doctor. The Graingers approved the plan, but the doctor admonished him not to spoil his life that way.

"If Alma will consent," he said, "it will be my deepest joy."

But when he came to Alma and told her his plan, she refused. "I cannot be so selfish," she said.

Later Clara Coney came to visit, and the two talked over Edwin's proposal. "Jesus said, 'It is more blessed to give than to receive.' " Clara held Alma's hand as she spoke: "Did you ever realize that if no one would ever receive, no one would ever have the blessing of giving? Will you deny Edwin the blessing of giving? You also have something to give—love and gratitude."

At last Alma decided. She would marry Edwin McKibbin. The wedding would take place the day after school closed.

Graduation, the great event of the year, arrived. Alma lay by the window in the gathering twilight and watched the students, the faculty, and the class—her class—go by. The darkness deepened, but an even gloomier pall of darkness settled over her.

All the things she had hoped to be and do rose up before her and seemed to mock her. She felt her mother's sorrow and her father's bitter disappointment that she could not carry out the plans and dreams they had for her. When she thought of her sisters, her heart broke. She cried in agony, "Oh, why, when I wanted so much to help them, should this affliction come upon me?"

In that dark hour her faith in the goodness of her heavenly Father grew weak. A wild desire to scream welled up within her—a desire to scream until her strength was gone. But she knew that if she did so, she would go into a convulsion and become unconscious and might die. She had been warned that she must always try to control herself, or the results would be very serious.

Suddenly the words of Job came to her mind out of the darkness. "What? shall we receive good at the hand of God, and shall we not receive evil?" Poor Job! He lost everything. Even his wife and his friends added to his grief. Yet he held fast his faith in God. Why should she doubt the goodness of God? Alma began to pray that God would give her a spirit of cheerful submission to His will. At once she began to plan to be a cheerful, happy invalid and resolved that Edwin should remember only her smiles, not her tears.

With that resolution having been made, it seemed that the room filled with a beautiful pearly light, and she heard music—soft, beautiful music that soothed her whole being.

"Oh, my dear," Mrs. Grainger said, entering Alma's room, "I should have left a light for you." Then she paused. "But you did not need a light—your face is beaming."

One of Alma's favorite passages that she memorized and repeated over and over to herself was from *Thoughts From the Mount of Blessing*, page 10: "The trials of life are God's workmen, to remove the impurities and roughness from our character. Their hewing, squaring, and chiseling, their burnishing and polishing, is a painful process; it is hard to be pressed down to the grinding wheel. But the stone is brought forth prepared to fill its place in the heavenly temple."

Alma's wedding day arrived, a beautiful May day. Alma was dressed in her robe and sitting in a reclining chair bolstered with pillows, as her friends wheeled her to a place beside Edwin. Roses and sweet peas filled the room with beauty and fragrant odors.

Edwin's brother and sister, the Grainger family, and Clara Coney attended. Before the wedding ceremony began, President Grainger stepped up to Alma and presented her a diploma with these words, "My wife has always said that a girl should finish her education before she is married. Unavoidably you have missed some months of your course, but because of your extracurricular activities, especially your Sabbath School work, the board of Healdsburg College feels free to grant you this diploma."

R. S. Owen, the Bible teacher at the college, performed the marriage ceremony. No two people ever took such solemn vows full of such meaning as Alma and Edwin took that day. "In sickness or in health, in adversity or prosperity." Elder Owen, like a fond father, prayed for the blessing of God on His dear children.

But where were the guests? Overcome by their emotions, they had slipped out of the room to weep together over a bride doomed to die. When they recovered their composure, they returned with smiles and kind wishes to see the couple off on their wedding trip—a short journey of three blocks down the street. The bridegroom and his brother Wynford carried the cot on which the bride lay to her new home.

Upon their arrival at the home the couple had chosen, Marian, Edwin's sister, opened the door and welcomed the couple. She stayed with them as their housekeeper, caring for their needs in a most unselfish manner.

For two months the bride knew no cares, no perplexity—only peace, contentment, and a great happiness. Edwin's sister, Marian, always thoughtful and kind, cared tirelessly for her new sister-in-law. Wynford, now a member of the new household, helped every way he could and always wore a cheerful smile.

But suddenly a shadow—small at first—fell on this happy home. It grew into a sense of impending calam-

Alma and Edwin McKibbin shortly after their marriage in the home of the president of Healdsburg College.

ity. Alma noticed that her beloved Edwin seemed to be ill. To her anxious questions he answered that it was only the summer heat. When cooler days came, he would be all right. But it was not so. At last he decided to go to St. Helena Sanitarium and have some tests.

A few days after Edwin had gone to St. Helena, one of the nurses came to call on Marian and told her that the examinations on Edwin were finished. "The doctor has discovered that your brother has tuberculosis in an advanced stage," she said.

Alma, who had been resting in her room, heard the nurse's remarks, since the door of her room had been left slightly ajar. She gasped at the nurse's words. It couldn't be true. Her Edwin in the advanced stages of—of— A merciful stupor came over her. She lay like one in a deep sleep the rest of the day and that night. The next day, the Sabbath, wore on before she became fully conscious of her surroundings.

That afternoon Mrs. Stafford, the wife of one of the professors, came to call. She had heard the news and had come to offer comfort to Alma. Then remembering Alma's love to be with God's people, she suggested that Alma attend the prayer group to be held that afternoon. "Two of the brethren will come and carry you over on a cot," she promised.

That afternoon the prayer meeting with friends of like faith did much to restore a degree of strength and courage to Alma's broken spirit. Then the professor's wife stood up and said, "We have all heard the report that has come from the sanitarium. You know, I have never believed that Sister McKibbin will never be well again. Last night I spent most of the night in prayer for her and for her husband, and I am deeply impressed that if we pray for her in faith, she will be healed. Do any of you have faith to pray with me?"

Brother McElhaney, uncle of one of the men who served as a General Conference president later, came over to Alma's cot and with Mrs. Stafford, the woman of great faith, knelt by Alma's bed. Each prayed a simple, sincere prayer. Then the woman took Alma's hand and said, "Sister McKibbin, in the name of Jesus of Nazareth, rise up and walk."

A profound stillness filled the room. My sister Alma sat up, swung her legs over the side of the bed, and stood up and walked.

"Praise the Lord! Praise the Lord!" came from every pair of lips in the room.

When Alma got back to her home, she sat down and wrote two letters, one to her mother and one to her husband. She had not been able to write one sentence for more than six months. A great joy, peace, and contentment filled her being.

Not long after this experience Edwin returned home. He seemed much improved and felt certain the doctors had made a mistake in their diagnosis. An optimism very common to tubercular patients seemed to grip Edwin, and Alma too felt encouraged.

When summer vacation time ended and a new school year began, Edwin entered his classroom eagerly. All went well until the rainy season started. Then the hacking cough returned. Alma became apprehensive the day the fever and coughing were so bad that he could not summon the strength to get up and go to school.

She went to tell Professor Grainger that Edwin did not feel up to meeting his classes that day. "But no doubt he will be there on the morrow," she added.

Professor Grainger smiled at Alma. "Then I think you will have to substitute for him today," he said.

"No!" she shook her head. "Not I. I couldn't possibly do that."

But Professor Grainger took Alma's arm and propelled her toward the classroom. He reassured her with a smile as he introduced her to the students. Alma McKibbin taught her first class that day, and she continued to teach for the remainder of the year.

The cold, damp winter weather in the Healdsburg area of California made Edwin's problem much worse. Relatives in southern California asked him to come and spend the winter with them. The rest and the warm, dry weather in San Pasqual Valley improved Edwin's health so much that the following year he was able to teach the full year at Healdsburg.

During that year Alma's health improved, and much to her joy she learned that a little one would soon come to gladden their hearts and home. Baby Lorin McKibbin could not have been loved or cared for more than he was. But the child was never strong. Perhaps he had inherited a weakness and frailty from both parents. Alma did all she could for the tiny lad, who suffered greatly those first few months of his life.

Then came another blow. The college board, under pressure from various patrons, asked Edwin to leave his teaching. It was thought to be too dangerous to have a tubercular teacher in the classroom.

What would the little family do? Edwin could not get another teaching position. No denominational provision existed for disabled workers in those days.

But the Lord opened doors once again in southern California. Relatives again invited Edwin and his little family as well to come and live with them. Two months after arriving at the southern California relatives' home, Baby Lorin breathed his last.

The parents, lonely and grief-stricken, consoled each other as best they could. They had had the little one with them only eleven months, and those months had been filled with suffering. Now he was asleep and would suffer no more. Alma, with tears streaming down her cheeks, said over and over again, "Angels will bear him to my arms in the resurrection morning and with his father we shall go where 'there shall be no more death, neither sorrow, nor crying, neither shall there by any more pain: for the former things are passed away.' "

Baby Lorin McKibbin brought joy to his parents for eleven months. Then he was laid to rest.

Conflict With Evil Spirits

Edwin and Alma stayed on with the relatives, but Edwin's health did not improve. He seemed to be failing fast. The couple had no income. Something had to be done. Gathering her strength and her courage, Alma decided to go to San Diego. There she found a position as housekeeper in the home of a dry-goods merchant. The woman of the house clerked in the store, and the twelve-year-old daughter needed special tutoring in history and arithmetic. Alma, who had thoroughly enjoyed teaching once she got into it, now had a job to do, helping this child as well as looking after the home.

Upon entering the room where she would stay, a feeling that she was not wanted in that place came over her. She shrugged it off and went about her tasks that evening; but when she returned to her room for the night, an awful fear pressed in on her. It seemed some power tried to push her from the room. Always having found comfort and courage from her Bible, Alma sat down to read. But as she read, the words were blurred, and before her eyes there appeared such phrases as "It's a lie." "Don't believe it." "Not a word of truth in it."

She slipped to her knees to pray, but a fear seized her. She must not close her eyes! In terror she looked about the room. It seemed like any other bedroom. When she got into bed, her hand trembled as she reached to turn off the light. It took a great deal of effort to plunge the room into darkness. She lay in her bed wide awake. Why did she feel so afraid? Why could she not sleep?

About two o'clock Alma dozed off but awoke in a few minutes in a cold sweat. The next night was the same, and the next. The fear and the lack of sleep told on her. She felt sick and unable to cope with the situation. She decided she would certainly have to leave. She would have to tell the lady of the house of her change of plans and ask to be relieved of her position immediately.

"Mrs. S," she began. But before she had time to tell the woman that she planned to leave, the woman blurted out, "What do you think of spiritualism?"

Alma opened her mouth to say, "I think it is of the devil." But she paused. Something seemed to impress her to be careful. "There are both good and evil angels," she said. "I believe spiritualism is the work of evil angels."

The woman then looked Alma straight in the eye and said, "I am a spiritualist! My father was the leader of 3000 spiritualists in this city."

Alma spoke up quickly, "I am sorry, but I cannot stay here. I am not well."

"Oh, Mrs. McKibbin, have you been disturbed?" the woman asked. "I am very sorry. You shall not occupy that room another night. I will make a bed for you in the parlor. Please, you must not go away. We like you. We want you to stay with us." She paused a moment and then went on. "No one has been able to sleep in that room since a drunken father struck his sick boy and he died. The father was never punished; so the boy's spirit will not allow anyone to rest in that room. I have no other bedroom. I had hoped you could sleep there. I have watched your face, and you gave no indication you were not sleeping. But you shall not stay there another hour. I will go right now and make a bed in the parlor for you."

"Oh, no, Mrs. S, you need not do that," Alma assured her. "Now that I know why I have been disturbed, I will ask God to take the evil spirit out of the room.''

The woman's eyes filled with tears. ''I wish you would ask Him to take all the evil spirits out of the house. My father's spirit is a good one and helps me, but there are others!'' She shook her head sadly.

''*You* must do that!'' Alma spoke quickly. ''This is your home. But while I am here, the bedroom is mine. I am God's child, and He will protect me from evil spirits if I ask Him. I did not know how to pray before you told me why the evil spirit disturbed me.''

Alma felt that the honor of God's name was at stake. It had to be demonstrated that He was more powerful than Satan and all his evil angels. That day Alma did only the work absolutely necessary. She spent most of the time out on the back porch, praying and reading her Bible. She asked God to increase her faith and by His mighty power to remove the evil angel from her room. When bedtime came, she knelt by her bed and prayed that He would help her to sleep, for she needed her rest. Alma rose from her knees and got into bed. That night she fell asleep quickly and awoke in the morning much refreshed.

Soon after this experience the family moved to a home next door to the mother of the dry-goods merchant's wife. Alma accompanied them. She learned that séances were held regularly at the mother's home. One evening Mrs. S told Alma that the medium at the séance that night had received a message that if she would fast and give herself to the influence of the spirit of a departed artist, she would be given the power to paint the portrait of the spirit of a departed friend. The medium had decided to start her fasting immediately. She remained at the home next door. Days went by. The medium painted some funeral wreaths—but no portraits. Other members of the spiritualist group began to fear for the woman. She lay in a room completely void of light or fresh air. She ate and drank nothing. She kept imploring the spirit to come with light and let her paint his portrait. Nothing happened.

Her spiritualist friends begged her to take some nourishment. But she refused. Finally the friends implored Alma to go to the woman and persuade her to give up her fasting and eat.

Alma prayed about the matter and then decided to go. When she entered the darkened room, she exclaimed, "You must let in the blessed sunshine and fresh air. Throw open the windows and doors." And she did just that. Then she requested that some hot soup be prepared.

When the windows and doors had been opened and the fresh air and sunlight filled the room, Alma spoke quietly to the medium. "Don't you want to live, my friend?"

The medium nodded her head.

"But you are going to die if you do not eat. To commit suicide is a great sin. You must eat and live."

"Please bring me the warm soup," Alma called to one standing nearby.

When the person brought the bowl of soup, the woman drank it eagerly. She looked up at Alma and smiled. Within a couple of days she was well and up and ready to return to her home.

After this experience the family for which Alma worked treated her with a great deal of warm respect and love. Always the lady of the house now referred to her as "my friend" or "my companion" or "my daughter's teacher."

Alma eagerly tried to teach the family the Bible truths. They never objected. They listened, but they seemed unable to comprehend. Soon the husband's business began to fail, and he lost everything. The family could no longer hire a housekeeper, and Alma had to go.

The night before she left, as the family sat at the table, the lady of the house began looking toward the parlor in such a way that Alma felt convinced she was seeing spirits.

"What do you see in the parlor?" the husband asked.

"Oh, I see a boat on a stream. A baby in the boat is playing with flowers. A man is holding the oars ready to push off from shore. They are both looking at you, Mrs. McKibbin. They do not want to go without you. Do turn around, Mrs. McKibbin. Don't you see them?"

"No," Alma answered, turning to look, "I see nothing but the furniture."

Then Mrs. S, who had never seen Alma's husband, described him perfectly, even to the tie he was wearing.

Alma insisted that she could see nothing but the furniture in that room. She prayed constantly while the woman told her about the boat and the child and the man in the boat. How she wished she could leave that house that very night, but she knew the angels of the Lord would be with her through those dark hours.

What Will You Have Me Do?

Always anxious to find someone who promised help for those afflicted with tuberculosis, Alma was overjoyed to hear about a physician in Los Angeles who seemed to be having a great deal of success in the treatment of the disease. She took Edwin to the city and found a place for him to stay with a good Adventist family. She herself began to search for work.

The new treatment did not help. Edwin now seemed beyond human help. The elders gathered around him and prayed. He himself believed he would get well. There was no need for him to remain in the city; therefore he returned to San Pasqual, where his sister Marian lived, while Alma searched for a job in Los Angeles so they could finish paying the bills that had mounted up.

Edwin wrote cheery letters to Alma—letters full of plans for reentering God's work. And Alma dared to hope that it might be true. But, alas, a letter arrived one day, not from Edwin, but from Marian. "You had better come home at once. Edwin is failing fast," it read.

The afternoon train carried Alma back to her husband. He lay on a couch in his sister's home, burning with fever. When Alma walked into the room, he tried weakly to raise his head and smile at her, but a violent fit of coughing left red blood stains on the cloth he held over his mouth. A few days later he had a severe hemorrhage.

"You thought you were selfish to let me take you to care for you, but I have proved to be the selfish one," he said weakly after a severe coughing spell. Then he added, "How strange are the ways of God. Today Professor Grainger, who is now an old man, sails away to begin work in a foreign land; and I, a young man, must give up life and its hopes to serve before it is well begun."

Another pause. And gathering strength he repeated as his last testimony, " 'I know that my redeemer liveth, and that he shall stand at the latter day upon the earth: and though after my skin worms destroy this body, yet in my flesh shall I see God.' "

The end came on November 4, 1896.

Alma had lost her dear one. She had lost her child. She had no home, no money, and very little strength. Then she thought of Edwin's words of courage: "I know that my redeemer liveth," and of the text "Casting all your care upon him; for he careth for you."

The Johnsons—father, mother, and six children ranging in age from seven to seventeen—opened their home to Alma. The oldest boy attended college at Healdsburg, while the two youngest—twins—a boy and a girl, had not yet started school.

The Adventist Church at this time had become interested in and agitated over the subject of church schools. Sister White, who had gone to Australia, sent letters back in which she implored the brethren to establish schools for our own children and youth. She even gave directions concerning the subjects to be taught. True education, she said, "is the harmonious development of the physical, the mental, and the spiritual powers"— not the training and development of the mind only, as most educators thought.

In other counsel she had written, "Bring your children to the simplicity of the word, and they will be safe. This Book is the foundation of all true knowledge. . . . God's word must be made the groundwork and subject matter of education."

Cont. next page

45

Alma and Mrs. Johnson discussed these statements as well as others that appeared in the *Review*. One day Mrs. Johnson suggested, "Why not try them out by teaching the twins and their little cousin?"

As an experiment the parlor of the Johnson home became a schoolroom. Three pupils met with Alma as the teacher every day. Not having any prepared textbooks and wishing to follow the instructions of Ellen G. White, Alma busied herself preparing a primer based on the first chapter of Genesis. This book became not only a reader but a Bible textbook and a nature book as well. To the astonishment of the parents and the teacher, within six short months the children were reading *Our Little Friend* and had committed to memory several of the psalms.

The *Review and Sabbath Herald* now carried weekly an article by Ellen G. White or by teachers Magan, Sutherland, Cady, or others. The members of the church read them and became deeply stirred with the message presented. The church members in San Pasqual Valley decided to follow the plan of education as outlined by the servant of the Lord. They had the schoolroom facilities, and they asked Alma McKibbin to be the teacher of the eight-grade school.

The idea scared her. She knew she was not a good disciplinarian. And she wanted time to learn how to make the Bible the groundwork of each subject. She did not feel at all qualified to teach.

But no one else could be found to teach the school. They insisted that Alma take over.

"Impossible!" Alma said. "I cannot take on eight grades." She felt completely overwhelmed by the task. There was only one thing to do—get away.

Like Jonah of old, Alma left the Johnson home, where she had been living, and went to Los Angeles to look for a housekeeping job. But all the while she was there she felt troubled and was not happy. The questions kept ringing in her ears, "Why am I here? Why am I not teaching?"

Alma had not let her friends know where she was working. Each Sabbath she attended church and then slipped quietly out and went home. However, one Sabbath the visiting minister noticed her and recognized her and wrote her a note, which he asked the usher to give her. The note read: "The church members at Centralia wish to start a church school and have asked me to get a teacher for them. Please remain after the service. I want to talk to you about it."

Alma waited until the last hymn had been announced; then she quietly slipped out of the church and went home. She did the same thing the next Sabbath.

On Sunday evening while she was preparing the evening meal for the family, Elder Snyder, with a delegation from the Centralia Church, came to call on her. Elder Snyder had asked an usher to follow her at a discreet distance when she had left the church the day before. The usher had told Elder Snyder the house address where she worked. The delegation pleaded with Alma long and earnestly to come and teach the church school.

"If I knew how to teach a church school, you would not need to ask me," she said. "I would be pleading with you for the privilege. The task is spiritual work. The principles are so different from public school teaching that I do not know how to carry them out, and there is no one to teach me. There are no textbooks of any kind, no course of study, no educational leaders, no one to give a bit of advice or counsel. Do you know, Elder Snyder, how a church school should be conducted?"

"No. I am a minister; but you are a teacher, and the Lord will help you and show you how this great and important work should be done."

"You must excuse me now," Alma said, looking at the clock. "The family is waiting, and I must serve the meal."

The delegation got up to leave. "I will come for your answer in the morning," Elder Snyder said.

"Please, don't come again," Alma said firmly. "You

Alma McKibbin organized the first Seventh-day Adventist church school in western United States at Centralia, Orange County, California, in 1897.

have my answer now. Do believe me when I say I do not know how and would fail if I tried it."

After her evening work had been completed, Alma went to her room and to bed. She could not sleep. Through the long dark night she wrestled with the problem. There were so many difficulties. Then it seemed that the presence of God was being withdrawn from her, and the room grew darker and darker. She felt alone—and lost! All night Alma struggled with the problem. At length when the dawn came, she gave up; but it was a sorry surrender. "Dear Lord," she said, "I will try. I can but fail."

A few weeks later Alma arrived at Buena Park at nightfall. There was no one at the station to meet her. To the weary and apprehensive girl Buena Park seemed to be in the middle of the Sahara Desert. No rain had fallen for two years. After a long wait at the little station she saw a two-wheeled cart drawn by a bony horse come in sight. In the cart sat a venerable-looking old gentleman, who invited her to "climb in." She then learned that she was to board and room at his home. Upon her arrival the man's wife looked Alma over critically. Then, arms akimbo, she said, "You won't last two weeks. No one can control some of these Centralia boys."

"Control"—the very thought struck terror to Alma's heart.

Later in the evening the little girl of the family inquired, "Will we have vertical?" Vertical was a system of penmanship that had come into use in the public schools not long before.

"Yes, we shall have vertical," Alma replied although she had never seen a specimen of vertical. She asked the little girl for a copybook, and that evening she learned to write and to teach the vertical method of writing.

When the school board met, they told her that because of the drought they could pay her only $15 a month and board. The church had only sixty members, and most were in straitened circumstances.

"Do not use public school books that teach evolution or have myths or fairy tales in them. Do not double grades, and above all things do not get behind the public schools in any subject. If you do, the children will want to go back to the public school," the spokesman for the board told her.

On Monday morning Alma started off to the school, a little room built onto the rear of the church. Because of lack of funds the room had never been finished. A twelve-inch board painted black served as a blackboard. The school board had been able to procure ten double seats that had been discarded by a public school. The stove smoked. A tin pail and dipper served as the drinking fountain.

That first morning Alma had to arrange seating in the ten double seats for 30 girls and boys. There were nine grades in that small room. The one ninth grader was a year older than the teacher.

"Our readers that we have used have nothing but myths and fairy tales in them. What do you intend to have us read from?" one of the students asked.

"We'll use *Our Little Friend,* the *Gospel Primer,* the little book called *Christ Our Saviour,* and the Bible," Mrs. McKibbin told her pupils.

Every night, seated in a cold, small, upstairs room in the northwest corner of the house, Alma wrote out two Bible lessons. One lesson was for grades 1 to 4, the other for grades 5 to 9. She also outlined a nature lesson each night. One of the students who loved nature roamed the countryside on Sundays seeking specimens for the teacher to use in the nature classes.

In that first school there was no library, no equipment of any kind—not even a map. The teacher had the class make relief maps on the ground in the school yard. The boys dug out oceans, rivers, lakes, and bays and then heaped up mountain ranges.

The lady of the house where Alma boarded seemed to look forward to the day when Alma would fail as a teacher at the Centralia school. Each morning when she came down to breakfast, the woman would ask, "Are you really going to try it another day?"

And Alma, with a smile, replied, "Yes, one more day. We live only one day at a time, you know."

October passed, November followed and passed, and December came. About the middle of the month Alma came down with a severe cold. She could hardly speak. That mile walk to school through the sand—with the Santa Ana wind blowing, causing the air to fill with dust—became almost unbearable. One morning about ten o'clock her voice failed. She could not utter one word. The pupils were allowed to pack up their books and go home. Christmas vacation started that day.

The Johnsons, who had been so kind to Alma and invited her to their home after Edwin's death, had once more asked her to visit them, and to spend the vacation time at their home in Escondido. However, when she arrived at their place Alma went to bed immediately. Six weeks passed before she could return to school.

Mrs. Johnson wrote to the Centralia school board and told them of Alma's illness. One day, much to Alma's surprise, she received an avalanche of letters from the folk in and around Centralia. Evidently Mrs. Johnson had written berating them for their treatment of their teacher. Now they were apologetic and remorseful because of their lack of appreciation and their indifference to her needs.

Upon returning to the school, Alma found the schoolroom had been plastered, blackboards had been made in the plaster, a new stove had been set up, and more windows had been made in the room. The school board had now arranged for her to board with a family living near the school. In her room she had a heater. She had also the wonderful privilege of being served breakfast in bed. That first evening after her return from the Johnsons she found a beautiful blue dressing gown in the closet. Such luxury! In the days that followed there were no disciplinary problems.

Meeting New Challenges

At the close of the school year in Centralia, my sister Alma received a call to attend camp meeting in Stockton, now in the Northern California Conference, and lead out in the primary division. While there at the camp meeting, she met Professor M. E. Cady, who had just been appointed president of Healdsburg College. He informed her that she had been chosen to teach the first four grades in the church school at Healdsburg, and the leaders wished to have her attend a summer school being held for church-school teachers.

Realizing that her work at the Centralia church school fell far short of the ideal and that she had much to learn about how to carry out the principles of Christian education, she arrived at Healdsburg eager and ready to begin a summer's training period.

However, the night before summer school began Professor Cady called her to his office and told her that he had to leave the next morning on a promotion tour for the college. "Professor E. S. Ballenger will be the principal for the summer school," he said. "And since you, Alma, will be the only one present who has ever taught church school, you will be Professor Ballenger's assistant and will teach methods in the common branches."

"Oh, no! I cannot do that," Alma answered.

But the next day Alma and eleven other persons met together to begin their thirteen weeks of intensive training. Not one of the summer school students, with the exception of Alma, had ever taught. Most of them had been out of school for several years. But they were all earnest and sincere and very humble.

Alma studied harder than any of the others, for she had to stand before the class as the teacher. Each evening she spent long, long hours preparing outlines for the day ahead. She used material gleaned from Mrs. White's writings, which became invaluable for instruction to the teachers that summer.

Professor Ballenger, a science teacher, presented outlines for nature lessons.

God blessed the summer school and students. They have often spoken of the times when they gathered together to pray, when God's Spirit seemed to come down to them and give them strength and courage and increase their faith.

At the close of summer school each person took the examination and received a note of commendation. Each one received a copy of the course of Bible study that had been made out during the summer. This consisted merely of a subject and Bible references. But it had taken many hours of work for Alma to accomplish it. Each teacher promised to write his or her own lessons for that coming school year. However, before long it became evident that the lessons were not being written out. The teachers felt their inadequacies and their lack of time.

When school began in September, Alma stood before her class of students. She had had all nine grades at the Centralia school. Here she had but four grades. Now this seemed like play. For two weeks Alma stood before the little ones in the first four grades and felt it was almost too good to be true. But at the beginning of the third week, right in the middle of the morning session, Professor Cady came to her classroom door. "Alma," he said, "we need you to take over the four upper grades. The teacher received a cablegram from Australia, and he had to leave immediately. Of course, we have a teacher for your room. Come with me."

Alma hesitated. She had had no preparation time for lessons. And here she was being ushered into a room full of boys and girls—fifty of them. She hardly heard the introduction Professor Cady made, when he turned and left her in the room full of children, most of whom she did not know.

One of the older boys in the room stood up and intimated that if Mrs. McKibbin were qualified to teach she should be able to explain some Bible statements that they could not understand. "One question," he said, "is about the resurrection. How can the resurrection be possible, for a dead body turns to dust and becomes a part of the earth as it was in the beginning. And sometimes a body is eaten by wild animals. What about that?"

Alma quickly sent up a silent prayer for divine help. Then noticing two students in the room who had been in her Sabbath School class seven years before, she smiled and asked, "Why, I see John and Nellie in the class, do I not? How strange that I should recognize them." She smiled at the two. "There is not a particle of matter in their bodies, nor in mine so far as that is concerned," she said to the class, "that was there when we knew each other seven years ago. Identity, you see, does not depend upon matter but upon personality and character. The only thing we can take to heaven is character. We shall have new bodies—a body that is new, incorruptible, immortal; one that will never know sickness, pain, or death."

The questioner sat down, and the students all seemed satisfied with the teacher's answer. They settled down to study and enjoy the rest of the school year. Alma had proved herself to be observant, calm, and ready to answer her students' questions to the best of her ability.

On Sundays Alma spent most of the day preparing and planning her classes for the following week. One Sunday not long after starting her work at the Healdsburg school, the ringing of her doorbell interrupted her work. Upon opening the door she found her mother and father standing there with a little boy.

In a moment she embraced Mother and Father Baker and then stooped down to look into the eyes of the little boy. Then she took him in her arms.

"Lonnie! You must be Lonnie!" she said, and then she held him at arm's length.

I was that little boy! Alonzo Lafayette Baker, Jr., but six years old. I was the youngest in the family. And just the age, I learned later, that her own little Lorin would have been had he lived. My sister Alma was twenty-two years my senior.

Mother explained to Alma that for some time her health had been failing. She hoped that by coming from Colorado to a lower altitude she would recover. The following year Grandmother came to California also, and Alma took her in. She had lost her memory and often became bewildered and homesick. The doors of the house had to be kept locked, for Grandmother would wander away searching for her home— Colorado.

How Alma struggled to keep together the family that had come to her. There was Mother, who never did regain her strength. There was Grandmother, bewildered and sickly. There was Father, who had no more use for Christianity and Seventh-day Adventism than he had had when Alma had been a child. One thing he did seem to admire was the fact that she had become a teacher—a teacher who was well thought of at Healdsburg. Then there was I, Lonnie, a live-wire little boy who never had a moment to sit still and think. But I loved my big sister Alma. She had taken me to heart, and I in turn loved and adored her.

How we ever managed financially those years is a mystery. My sister Alma received $30 per month during the school year—nine months. A relative did send her $5 a month to take care of Grandma. But somehow she managed to care for us all on $330 a year.

After being with us at Healdsburg for two years,

Little Brother Lonnie came to Alma at the age of six, just the age her baby Lorin would have been had he lived.

Father Baker decided to leave and go back to Colorado. He had informed us that he had only come out to bring Mother Baker and me. He really did not wish to remain any longer with an "Advent-religious-crazy wife." He left my mother and me there with Alma. Mother never saw him again. My other two sisters, who still lived in Colorado at the time, showed him no love or respect. When they learned that Alma prayed continually for our father, they wrote: "Alma, why waste your breath and your time praying for that ornery old man?"

Alma answered always, "The fifth commandment says, 'Honour thy father.' I would be dishonoring my heavenly Father if I disobeyed His command to honor my earthly father."

Pressures at home with Mother and Grandmother ill and with a young boy to look after made it necessary for my sister to find someone to help with the home from time to time. Grandmother fell and injured her hip. She never walked again, and Mother had a stroke and became paralyzed. From then on she was confined to bed or a wheelchair until her death.

Since there was no money to hire help, Alma gratefully accepted the services of a neighbor who dropped in two or three times during the day to do what was necessary for the two invalids.

Teachers in church school were still begging for Bible lessons. Sometimes Bible classes were not taught in the schools because there were no prepared lessons.

My sister Alma felt that if the Bible were not taught, then all efforts to establish church schools were in vain. Professor Cady talked to her often about the need, and he urged her to write the lessons.

But when would she find the time? Surely she had more to do now than human strength could endure. But always the Lord gave her strength for the day. In gratitude for this she felt compelled to take on the task of writing Bible lessons.

She had never written a book. But she now began. She authored the material, proofread it, had it printed at the Healdsburg College Press at her own expense, and was her own business manager.

Orders for the books came in faster than the books could be finished. Signatures had to be taken as they came off the press, and Alma herself put the first twelve signatures together with a shoe string. Then she walked to the post office after the teaching day, mailed the requested lessons, and trudged back home to look after the home duties.

One evening in December she came home later than usual, having stopped at the college press on her way home from school to pick up some of the Bible books. She had received that day, she said, a large order for the books, from faraway Australia. The books had to be mailed immediately.

Although only eight years old, I did what I could to help her see to the comforts of Mother and Grandmother and then get dinner ready. "I'll feed Mother," I offered, knowing that Grandmother would have to be fed as well.

The Healdsburg College Press printed the first Bible textbooks authored by Alma McKibbin. Standing in foreground is A. F. Haines, teacher of printing. Seated to right of post is Alma McKibbin reading proofs of the Bible books.

Alma gave me a smile and a hug. "Thanks, Brother. You are a real help to me. I'll feed Grandma. She doesn't seem to recognize anyone else."

Supper over at last, the dishes washed, and the two invalids made as comfortable as possible for the night, Alma sat down to wrap the books and address the package.

"Brother, please keep the fire going in the stove and put a lighted lamp in the window for me," she said. "It will be late when I get home. I just hope the postmistress doesn't give me a hard time. She hates to be bothered after supper, especially with foreign mail."

I watched her start out in a slow drizzling rain with a chilly wind blowing. Then I went to sit with Mother. Hours later, my sister Alma returned. She had to awaken me, for I had fallen asleep while sitting at the table. The postmistress had made her wait until after eight o'clock before she would serve her, she said. Then when the lady saw the package was to go to Australia, she became very angry. Then she learned what the package contained and that the books had been written by Alma herself. Apparently the woman had a great deal of respect for authors. After that the postmistress became a good friend and was eager to help.

A few weeks after this experience one of our sisters came from Denver to be with us. Now there would be someone at home with Mother and Grandmother when my sister Alma and I were at school. There would also be someone at home to care for and direct me after school when Alma was not at home. Our sister did the housework at home as well as the fine laundry for guests at a nearby resort. The money she earned helped with the household bills.

We had been living in a small three-room house in Healdsburg. But that small house made a home, a home full of love.

One day my sister Alma came home with the news that she had rented the Ellen G. White house. There were four large bedrooms upstairs, two bedrooms downstairs, and a sitting room, a dining room, and a kitchen. At the rear of the house a laundry room and a woodshed had been built on. All that rented for $8 a month.

"What is Mrs. White going to do?" I wanted to know.

"Well, Brother," my sister Alma began, "Sister White is not a young woman anymore. Now that she has returned from Australia, where she went before you and Mother came to live with me, her son and other people who advise her think that she should be near the sanitarium in St. Helena, where she can get medical help if and when she needs it. She has already found and purchased a place called Elmshaven and will be going there to live. It's near the sanitarium."

We moved into the big house. It had been only a cottage with two bedrooms when the Whites had

The Bible textbook signatures were gathered and tied together with a shoestring. They became known as the "shoestring" Bible books. Alma McKibbin also kept a book of remembrance, which contained the names of all her students throughout the years.

purchased the place. Because of the need of more room for her secretaries and other helpers, the cottage had been enlarged and a second story added. But now two sisters, Grandma, Mother, and I moved into the big house. What a place for a boy to roam around—garden space, orchard, and lots of room to play in.

Two of the bedrooms my sister Alma rented out. Whenever Mrs. White came to Healdsburg, she always came to our home that had been hers. How she loved the place! The first time she came, she asked to go out and see the orchard. There were two and a half acres of orchard around the house. I followed my sister Alma and Mrs. White out into the yard. Mrs. White stopped to remark about the great pine tree in the yard. How it had grown since she had gone to Australia! Then she looked down at all the needles on the ground. "We'll never see anything like that in the new earth," she said to my sister. "Nothing will ever fade or wither there, and there will be no more death." At those last few words her voice became stronger and more vibrant, and her whole face seemed to glow with a serene happiness.

My eyes watched every move of this short, stout little woman as she and my sister went on to the orchard. Sister White lightly stepped from the top of one furrow to another. She never seemed to touch the ground as she walked. As the three of us walked, Sister White's eyes lighted up as she saw the trees laden with fruit. She knew every tree and when it was planted.

Another time when Mrs. White came to our home in Healdsburg, she asked if Alma would take her through the house. As usual, I tagged along behind but as close as I could without being in the way. My sister Alma first took Mrs. White to the laundry room that Mrs. White had had built on the back of the house. Opening from the laundry room was the bathroom. Mrs. White laughed when she looked into the bathroom. "Way out here! But it really was a great convenience after all."

My sister Alma smiled and agreed. "We'll go upstairs now if you wish to," she said.

Alma's mother, sister, and brother Lonnie came from
Denver to make their home with Alma in California. Back
row: Alma and Lonnie. Front row: Mother Baker and
Alma's sister.

"Oh, I see you have put a handrail on," Mrs. White remarked as she started up the stairway. "I should have had that when I lived here. It's a great help in going up the stairs."

At the top of the stairs Alma turned to open a door on the right. "This is my room," she said.

"Oh!" Mrs. White smiled. "It was my room when I lived here." She walked past Alma into the room. "And you have your desk just where I had mine. The light is good here." With that light, floating step she walked over to the desk between the two big windows. She put her hands on the desk, then looked up and said, "I finished *Patriarchs and Prophets* here."

There were papers on my sister's desk, and Mrs. White asked, "What are you writing?"

Quietly my sister Alma answered, "I am trying to prepare some little Bible lesson books for the children in the church school."

"Why, this is going to be a very good book, Sister McKibbin," Mrs. White said. "Would you mind letting me have these signatures? I'd like to look them over."

Alma gathered them up and handed them to Mrs. White.

What would she do with that handful of signatures? I wondered as I watched her.

She felt around on her skirt, found a large concealed pocket, and slipped the signatures into it.

Once more Mrs. White put her hand on the stair handrail and tripped lightly downstairs. At the foot of the steps she turned to Alma and asked, "Sister McKibbin, how are you getting along financially?"

"Why, don't worry about me," my sister answered. "We manage to make ends meet."

"Sister McKibbin," Mrs. White smiled at my sister and went on, "if ever there should come a time when things are hard for you and you find it hard to send the money, you just write to my secretary and tell him that this month Sister White said you were not to send the rent."

The large two-storied house in Healdsburg rented from
Ellen G. White.

To my knowledge my sister never took advantage of
that offer; but to me, a young boy, hearing those kind
words gave a wonderful insight into Mrs. White's
character. Although some of the testimonies borne to
people sounded harsh, I knew that Mrs. White was not
harsh but a kind, generous and thoughtful person.

The time came for her to return to Elmshaven. My
sister and I walked to the yard gate with her and her son
Willie, who had come with her. Mrs. White stopped at
the gate. ''Oh, look at that, Willie,'' she said, pointing
to the big rose geranium plant that grew by the gate. ''I
planted that rose geranium myself years ago. It is still
alive.'' Then she turned to my sister and asked, ''May I
have a leaf?''

My sister broke off a sprig and handed it to Mrs.
White. She took the bit of rose geranium with her. Later
Miss McEnterfer, one of her secretaries, told us that
Mrs. White had slept with the rose geranium leaf under
her pillow that night.

Through the years my understanding of and faith in
Mrs. White as a prophet of the Lord and as a woman, a
mother in Israel, a person genuinely interested in

people grew and strengthened. She lived what she taught, and she always found time to be pleasant and appreciative.

My sister Alma decided shortly after that visit from Mrs. White, when she had been so concerned about our welfare, that we should have a garden and grow vegetables. This would save money that we usually had to spend at the greengrocer's.

"You, Brother, will be head gardener," she said, laughing as she spoke. "I don't know anything about gardening, but Sister Critchlow, down the street, knows how to garden; and she said she would be willing to teach us how to raise lettuce, carrots, beets, turnips, potatoes, green beans, and—"

"Do we have to grow all those at once?" I asked, my enthusiasm for gardening already sinking.

However, within a few months the garden produced so much that our household couldn't use it all. I started peddling and selling vegetables to several families in Healdsburg. Depending on the season of the year, I was able to contribute to our family's household account $2.50 to $5 a month.

Lessons Learned

In the fall my sister and I canned or dried our abundant fruit crop. She bought a secondhand apple peeler and slicer, which I used to prepare apples by the boxful for making into applesauce or else for placing on trays to dry in the sun. The shelves in the basement soon held several hundred two-quart jars of applesauce, peaches, cherries, and plums. There were also several flour sacks full of dried apples stored away in that basement, as well as many glass jars full of shelled almonds and walnuts from our plentiful harvest. My sister developed in me, without my recognizing it at the time, a wholesome character trait—a fascination for productive work.

Early in the year 1908 a well-known denominational evangelist and revivalist of that era, Elder Luther Warren, came to Healdsburg College and to the Healdsburg Church community. To a boy of fourteen years who would be graduated from the eighth grade of the church school in June, Luther Warren—a tall, austere man who always wore a long down-to-the-ankle black coat—seemed to preach very long, somber sermons. He avowed in every sermon: "If Jesus should return to this world and to Healdsburg today, no more than one out of every twenty would be saved from the lake of fire." But he did bring about a real revival in the Healdsburg Church.

One evening at the supper table my sister said, "Elder Warren has called all parents to a special meeting tonight at the church. He said few Adventist parents are rearing their children in the fear of God. He will tell us in detail tonight where we are failing in our duty as parents. Please go to bed at nine o'clock if I am not home at that time, but just check on Mother and Grandmother to see that they are properly covered."

Throughout the evening I wondered what Elder Warren's message to parents could be about. But I had to wait until morning to find out. At breakfast time my sister placed her hand on my arm and said, "Brother, I have some news for you that may make you unhappy; nevertheless, I feel it my duty to carry out the instructions that Elder Warren gave us last night." She paused and then went on. "We must sell the rooster and the forty hens we have immediately."

"But—but—why? Why would Elder Warren make so outrageous a demand upon us?" I burst into a fit of angry tears.

"Because," replied my sister, "Elder Warren says parents will be held responsible by God if they allow their children to eat improperly and—"

"Wherever did Elder Warren get such a crazy idea as that?" I looked up defiantly at my sister.

She placed her hand over mine and said, "Elder Warren told us last night that when immature boys and girls eat too many eggs, those eggs cause their baser passions to be aroused."

"Baser passions? Baser passions? What in the world are baser passions?"

My sister's face blushed red, but she tried her best in her modest way to convey to me the import of Elder Warren's directive. Then she went on to say, "Mrs. White, a number of years ago, wrote that parents should be instructing their children how to shun the vices and corruptions of the age. She spoke about parents placing on their tables for their children to eat so much butter, eggs and meat. They are fed the very things that arouse

67

their animal passions," she said. "When parents have done all for their children that God has left for them to do, then parents can claim the special help that God has promised to give. Mrs. White wrote that in her second volume of the *Testimonies* in 1870. Later she wrote that 'those who live in new countries or in poverty-stricken districts where fruits and nuts are scarce, should not be urged to exclude milk and eggs from their dietary.' Brother, we have an abundance of fruit and nuts and vegetables too. We do not need eggs and I think we should get rid of our chickens."

I cried and protested the selling of our flock of forty-one chickens. I felt angry at Elder Warren.

My sister Alma cried with me. "I know you are heartbroken, Brother, but you must not be angry with Elder Warren. I feel I cannot jeopardize our having a home in the kingdom by being lax in caring for our bodies and by using an improper dietary."

The loss of forty laying hens was a considerable financial loss to our home, for we had been selling to neighbors several dozen eggs every week at 10 cents a dozen. This egg revenue often met our monthly rent of $8.00, which went to Mrs. White, the owner of the house and the land. Furthermore, our mother and grandmother, both invalids, loved soft-boiled eggs; and both my sister and I carried lunches to school each day with hard-boiled eggs to go with our sandwiches. Thus the sudden loss of our chicken flock constituted a financial crisis for us. I pointed out the financial dilemma we would be in minus our egg business.

My sister ended our discussion by saying, "Brother, when God's servant tells us that something we are doing should be stopped, we have no options. Obey we must. I pray God every day to show me how to support our family on my yearly salary, and He hasn't failed me yet."

That year Grandma passed away. She had reached ninety-two years of age but had been helpless and had suffered much for some time. Hers had been a long and useful life. And now we missed her. Soon after her death came another blow—Healdsburg College would be no more. The brethren decided to move the school to Angwin, California, where it became known as Pacific Union College. My sister Alma, although asked to move with the college and be on its faculty, felt that she could not take Mother there, where accommodations at the time were so primitive. We decided to remain in Healdsburg. Also the church needed someone to hold the members together after the closing of the school. My sister visited every member left behind and encouraged each one. She helped out in the Sabbath School and often took charge of the church service—there being no minister to pastor the flock.

The move of the college to Angwin and the decline in church membership brought financial problems to the Healdsburg Church. It had been for many years the second largest in membership in California, the Oakland Church being the largest. The Healdsburg board of elders decided the church could now no longer afford to employ a full-time custodian. They were forced to find someone who would accept a minimum salary. On a Sabbath morning the call was made for a volunteer to do the janitorial work.

I leaned over to my sister Alma, who always sat with me on the front row in church. "Maybe I could do the janitor work here," I whispered.

My sister placed a finger to her lips as she whispered back, "We must not talk in church."

The minute we left the church and had begun our long walk home, I brought up the idea again.

"You are too young to be trusted with all that work and responsibility," my sister replied with a note of finality in her voice.

But I had learned how to work, and I was not afraid of work. Besides, we needed the money. I could not get the idea out of my head, and that evening I pursued it again. "Sister," I said, "Bennie Grant and I could do that job together, dividing the money equally."

"Oh, Brother, Bennie is even younger than you are. Forget it. The church board would never consider two young boys!"

But two weeks later Bennie Grant, my special friend, and I had the janitorial job at the church. We each received the sum of $4 a month to be applied to our tuition in the church school. The tuition, by a strange coincidence, was $4 a month. Some time later my sister asked the head deacon if the boys were doing a good job. Both Bennie and I felt immense satisfaction when she told us the deacon had reported our work was most satisfactory.

That winter Elder J. N. Loughborough returned to Healdsburg. He who with Elder D. T. Bourdeau had first brought the message to California in 1868, and who had been preaching in Santa Rosa when the Bakers had come to California to see their relatives many years before, now came to encourage the church after it had lost so many members when the college moved. Elder Loughborough himself had been instrumental in founding the school in 1882. Now he hastened back to Healdsburg to give a series of sermons on early Adventism and report on the progress of the third angel's message around the world to encourage the dwindling Adventist group in Healdsburg.

The first Sabbath of Elder Loughborough's visit, a cold, rainy day, Bennie and I fired up the two huge stoves in the auditorium. Each six-foot-tall stove ravenously consumed the two-foot logs that we kept feeding them. We sat behind the stove in the rear of the auditorium when we were not stoking the fires. Thoughtlessly on this particular Sabbath we began to whisper to each other, and our conversation made us both stifle a snicker or two. Suddenly we realized a great silence had settled in the auditorium. Then a voice of doom spoke. "Lonnie Baker and Bennie Grant, you two boys should be ashamed of yourselves for laughing and whispering in the house of God on the Sabbath day. Where is your sense of reverence?"

Bennie and I were petrified as we looked around the stove and saw hundreds of pairs of eyes turned on us. Every member of the congregation had turned in his seat to look, we felt, with scorn and disdain at us. The minute the benediction had been pronounced we instantly disappeared into the basement of the church.

When we thought everyone had gone home, we came out of the basement only to find my sister Alma and Bennie's mother and two aunts talking together. My sister exclaimed as she burst into tears, "Brother, I have never felt so humiliated and disgraced in all my life as I am this moment." Bennie's mother added, "Bennie, you can walk the three miles home."

Bennie and I locked up the church. He walked home alone. My sister and I walked home, neither uttering a syllable all the way. The stinging rebuke of the day stayed with me for many years. Then it was forgotten after I grew up and matured. However, one day while at my desk as an editor of *Signs of the Times* at the Pacific Press in Mountain View, California, I received a letter with this notation in the left-hand corner: "If not called for in 10 days return to J. N. Loughborough, Sanitarium, California." The name Loughborough on that letter brought back to mind that cold, rainy Sabbath in Healdsburg some sixteen years before, when Bennie Grant and I had been rebuked in church for whispering. Elder Loughborough, I knew, had been retired for years. Now why was he writing to me? I tore open the envelope.

"Dear Lonnie Baker:" I read. "For some weeks now I have felt that I am nearing my last day in this life, so have been going over all my diaries to see if there is anything that I need to rectify in order to meet my Maker in peace on the Great Resurrection Day. In my diary for 1909 I found that in a series of sermons I gave in the Healdsburg Church I had too harshly rebuked Bennie Grant and you. As I read my exact words which I had said to you two boys, I was convinced that I had spoken altogether so severely and harshly that I am sure

Colonel Ben E. Grant, a graduate of both Pacific Union College and Loma Linda and later commander of the 47th hospital unit in World War II, who, with Lonnie, had been rebuked by Elder J. N. Loughborough.

you were humiliated before all the congregation. I have asked God to forgive me for treating you two boys that way. Now I hope that you and Bennie can also forgive me. Please send this letter on to Bennie, for I do not know where he is living now."

Yes, the rebuke had been hard to take; but to know that this man, this leader in God's work, felt the need to write me and ask forgiveness for his sharpness to me, a boy who had needed a reprimand, brought tears to my eyes.

Only a few weeks later John North Loughborough went to his rest. He awaits the coming of the Life-giver in the beautiful St. Helena cemetery where many other Adventist pioneers also rest.

All the while, my sister Alma and I remained in Healdsburg after the move of the college to Angwin. My sister spent untiring efforts to bring about a spirit of unity in the church. With the Holy Spirit working on the members along with the personal work that Alma did, many differences that had developed in the church were forgotten, and several new members were added.

The sister who had come from Colorado to help Alma care for our invalid mother and grandmother and me now decided to marry and start a home of her own. Because I could go no further in the nine-grade school in Healdsburg, Alma decided I should go to Pacific Union College. That left Alma alone with our bed-ridden mother.

Upon my arrival at the college in 1910, President C. W. Irwin informed me that my sister had written stating that I would require enough employment by the college to pay my tuition costs. "You know, of course," President Irwin went on, "that all students are required to work fifteen hours weekly for the school regardless of their family's financial status. That means you will have to work twenty-five hours above the fifteen. You see, your sister said she could pay only a minimal amount per month on your board, room, and tuition costs; therefore, you will have to work out the remainder."

"How many hours all together?" I asked.

"Forty hours," the president replied. "You will report to John Paap for your work assignment."

When I reported to the farm manager, he said with a laugh, "Lonnie, you will be 'chambermaid' to the horses, all eighteen of them!"

I soon learned the importance of my job. The only method of conveyance to the little town of St. Helena, eight miles from the college perched on top of Mount Howell, was by horse-drawn buses or freight wagons pulled by four horses. Those eighteen horses were our sole means of connection with the rest of the world. Each morning at 5:30 my work began at the barn, from where I fed the horses, curried and brushed them, and then harnessed them for the day. At 7:30 I went to breakfast in the college dining room. Classes occupied the rest of the morning. In the afternoon I cleaned out the individual horse stalls at the barn and wheeled the soiled straw bedding and the manure out behind the barn, from where it was eventually carted away to the garden to be used as fertilizer. I had to place fresh straw in the stalls and hay in the mangers, to unharness the horses as they came in after their day's work, and to feed them their grain. Also I had to inspect regularly the axles of all the horse-drawn vehicles and keep them well greased.

The second year at the college I worked at the sawmill. I rode the carriage that carried the logs back and forth as the logs were sliced into boards and dimension lumber. The college supplied much of the lumber used for the construction of a number of large buildings in the area.

Although I worked my twenty-five hours per week for 15 cents an hour plus the fifteen hours required without pay, by the end of the school year I always owed the college money. Therefore, I stayed on during the summer months. For five years I worked each summer, ten to twelve hours daily to keep my account with the school in the clear. There was never any cash paid to me, only credit on my college financial account.

My sister Alma wrote to me regularly to encourage me and assure me of her love. In one of her letters she sent word that Mother had finally passed away.

Not long after this Alma left Healdsburg and came to Pacific Union College. My sister and I found an old red farmhouse on the hill behind the school. She rented it. Now she took in my best friend, Ben Grant, who had come to college. We lived there with my sister Alma all through our college years. My sister taught in the Bible department and looked after Ben and me as if we were both her very own sons.

Whenever possible Professor Irwin invited Mrs. White to come and speak to the student body. One of her last visits was in the fall of 1914. She had been brought up the hill the night before she was to speak, for the trip up to the college drained her strength. In the morning Professor Irwin and Willie, Mrs. White's son, lifted her up the steps and brought her to the chapel. They helped her up to the desk, where she held on while her son, his arm about her, steadied and gave her support. I remembered vividly how she had seemed to fly lightly as she tripped down our garden path at the Healdsburg home years before. Now her steps were feeble and slow. She spoke. Her voice at first trembled slightly; but as she spoke, she articulated clearly, and a certain strength seemed to come into her being.

"Dear young people," she said, "I am so glad that God has once more permitted me to come and speak to you. I was young like you when God called me to His work. I put my armor on, and I have never taken it off. Young people, put your hand to the plow and never turn back. My work is almost done. My secretaries are busy gathering together the manuscript and the material for another book. I want to finish the series of books I started, the Conflict of the Ages Series, before I close my eyes in sleep. I help with the work as much as I can,

The Pacific Union College faculty in 1911-12. Alma McKibbin, front row right, taught Old Testament and Jewish History. G. W. Irwin, president and business manager of the college, is also in the front row, third from the right.

but my strength is not what it was once. But so long as I live, I will not take off my armor."

She talked not more than ten minutes. One would think not a soul was in that room while she spoke, such a quietness pervaded the room. Then when she had finished speaking, her son and President Irwin took her out onto the porch and put her in a chair. No one left the chapel. We sat there thinking of her words. She sat on the porch awaiting the arrival of her carriage. Then we heard her begin to sing. She seemed to forget entirely where she was. She sang, "Jesus is coming again, coming again. I have waited long, Jesus is coming again."

When her carriage came and she left the hilltop, President Irwin came into the chapel and dismissed us to our classes.

On February 13, 1915, Mrs. White had an accident in her home at Elmshaven. Word came to us at the college that she had fallen at the door of her room and had broken her hip. She lived and worked those last five months even though ill, finishing up as best she could the work that had been assigned to her. "I do not want to leave an unfinished work," she repeated over and over to those who came in to minister to her. Then her final words: "I know in whom I have believed." In July of that year she fell asleep to await the second coming of her Lord.

The following year both Ben and I graduated from the four-year college course. Ben went on to medical college, while I became a ministerial intern in the Northwestern California Conference.

The War Years

In March 1917 the Pacific Press in Mountain View, California, invited me to become one of the editors in the *Signs of the Times* editorial office. I accepted and moved to Mountain View. Although World War I had been raging for three years, the United States had been only indirectly affected. However, on April 6, 1917, the United States became definitely involved. Conscription came into full force. A number of my friends received the call to serve their country. One day a letter came to me from Woodrow Wilson, the President of the United States. The letter read: "Greetings: You are hereby ordered to report to the Commander of Fort Rosecrans, Coast Artillery Corps, San Diego, California, . . . for induction into the United States Army." This would mean my editorial career would be short-lived. No one knew how long the war would continue.

Immediately I wrote to my sister Alma, still at Pacific Union College, to tell her that I had been drafted and would be leaving soon for San Diego on a troop train. I would be serving in the Coast Artillery Corps.

A few days later my sister telephoned to me. She seemed greatly concerned over the fact that I would be in the Coast Artillery Corps. "Surely, Brother, you know you must tell the army you are a noncombatant." My sister pleaded with me to demand noncombatancy status when I arrived in San Diego.

When the train carrying 1000 draftees arrived in San Diego, we were transported to Fort Rosecrans and lined up for assignment. The first 250 men were assigned to Battery A. The second 250 to Battery B, the third to Battery C, and the fourth to Battery D. I was one of the 250 men placed in Battery C.

The sergeant major ordered Battery C to line up to be interviewed as to our various abilities. He began with all those in Battery C whose names began with A.

He finally came to the B's. "Alonzo Lafayette Baker," he boomed. At that name the draftees, all 249 of them in that battery, guffawed, and I felt every eye on me as I stepped forward.

"What have you ever done which will make you useful to this man's army?" the sergeant major asked in rather a cynical voice.

"I've done farm work, I've painted a house, I worked in a sawmill, I have a college education and—"

The sergeant major cut me off. "All that is not worth a _____ in the U.S. Army. Can you do anything practical?"

"Sir, in college I earned not only an A.B. degree with a history major, but I also received a certificate in stenography. I have also passed the U.S. Government civil service examination."

The sergeant major let out a whoop. "Colonel, sir," he called to the commander of Fort Rosecrans, who was standing nearby. "Colonel, sir, I have a prize package for Battery C. This Alonzo Lafayette Baker recruit can not only take shorthand dictation, but he can also use a typewriter without looking at the keys. He's passed his civil service exams."

The commander came over and called me out of the line. He questioned me at length and then called to the sergeant major: "Baker will bunk with Battery C, but he will work full time in my office."

I suddenly realized that because of the questioning of the sergeant major this job that had been assigned to me meant I would be exempt from carrying a rifle, daily drills, tiresome inspections, and all that. Much later I learned that my sister Alma had been praying earnestly for her boy, her brother Lonnie, that he would be able to stand firm and uphold the truths that she had tried to instill in him from childhood.

Upon reporting to work in the commander's office, I met two other young men working there. They were regular army enlistees, not draftees. The two men both enjoyed horse races; and the first weekend I was there, they planned to go to the races in Tijuana, Mexico. Much to their dismay one of the men found his name on the roster to report to work on Sunday.

"It's a lousy shame that one of us will be stuck in this office on Sunday when the horse races are on. Think of all the betting down there—and all the girls!" the one fellow exclaimed, while the other man frowned and swore.

Now I went to look at the roster. There was my name, Alonzo Lafayette Baker. I was scheduled for duty on Saturday! Duty on Saturday? That I felt I couldn't do. An idea struck me. Going to one of the young men, I said, "Hey, pal, want to switch places with me? I'm scheduled to work on Saturday. I'll be glad to change places with you and work on Sunday if you'd like to take my place on Saturday."

"Baker," the man replied, "you must be nuts to want to work on Sunday when you don't have to; but if you're that crazy, I'll take you up on your offer."

The following week we three worked out a schedule whereby I worked every Sunday and had every Sabbath off and the other two men had their Sundays free. Each Sabbath, with scores of other servicemen, I attended the Broadway Seventh-day Adventist Church.

One day one of the men in the office asked me what I did with myself on Saturdays.

"Oh, I go to church, the Seventh-day Adventist Church."

Both men looked at me in disbelief. "Now we know you are really nuts. Imagine choosing to go to church rather than have a big time in Tijuana." They shook their heads in dismay. They did not offer to change jobs back. I kept working on Sunday, and they worked on Saturday.

In the fall of 1918 the deadly plague of influenza spread across the world. It killed some 20 million people. In San Diego alone thousands of soldiers, Marines, and Navy personnel came down with the dreaded flu. Hospitals in San Diego were filled to overflowing, and morticians ran out of coffins.

For several weeks the flu had been doing its destructive work among the soldiers at Fort Rosecrans. Having from early childhood developed a strong body, thanks to my sister's thoughtful care of me and my diet, I thought I would be able to avoid the dreaded bug. However, I awoke one morning burning with fever. An army doctor ordered me to the base hospital immediately. Cots placed end to end in long lines took up every available square foot of space at the hospital. The narrowest of space separated one line of cots from another. The soldier on one side of me died on my second night in the hospital. The nurse pulled a sheet over the dead man's face and left him lying there. It was noon the next day before the corpse was moved out of the room.

Word soon made the rounds at the hospital that all cases that were destined to die would be moved out onto the screened veranda. Of course, the patients were not supposed to know this, but the word filtered through to us.

One night I had acute chest pains and found great difficulty in breathing. At four in the morning the doctor and nurse were called in to see me. The doctor ordered the nurse to have my chest cavity drained. This they did twice during that day. In the evening when the doctor made his rounds, he looked at me and said, "Private Baker, I am ordering you moved out to the veranda where you will have more room and fresh air."

"That means it is over for me!" I thought. I knew I

should write my sister Alma. But for a time unconsciousness took over. I came to about midnight. A volunteer nurse bending down to straighten my bedclothes smiled at me as I opened my eyes. With every breath I drew I felt a stabbing, searing pain in my chest. "Please," I begged the volunteer nurse, "please—could—I—have—a—a—pain—pill?" After each word sharp pains shot through me.

She wiped the perspiration from my forehead. I could see a tear in her eye as she told me she could give me nothing without doctor's orders. "I wish I could help you, but I must not without orders."

Then I remembered that when I had been a boy in Healdsburg and had suffered with a cold my sister Alma had used hot fomentation cloths, a Dr. Kellogg treatment. Although it had seemed that the hot cloths would scorch the skin off my chest, and I had always tried to resist the hot cloths, the pain had left soon after the treatment. If only my sister Alma were around now! Between painful breaths I asked the woman to bring me a half dozen hot water bottles filled with the hottest water she could find. I wanted them placed on my chest.

"My dear boy," the woman answered, "I wish I could, but I can't without an order."

Summing up all my strength and determination I ordered, "Well, I outrank you even though I am only a private. I still outrank a civilian. I order you to bring me the hot water bottles filled with hot water."

She brought the hot water bottles and put them on and around my chest.

When I saw the doctor and the nurse coming toward my cot early in the morning, I took the water bottles, now cold, and shoved them under the cot. Then I pulled the covers up around my neck. The nurse put the thermometer in my mouth and counted my pulse.

When she took the thermometer reading, she exclaimed, "Doctor, I can't understand it; this man's temperature reading last night was 107°, now it is down to 99."

The doctor looked at the chart. "The chart says he won't live till morning." He shook his head.

The next day, November 11, 1918, World War I came to an end by the signing of an armistice. Perhaps the end of the war boosted our morale and thus our resistance. It seemed this event had the effect of a shot in the arm. Within three days after armistice I returned to Fort Rosecrans.

The commander smiled when I walked into the office. "I'm glad you didn't die four nights ago," he said. "Now, if you and the other two men, with my help, will get busy typing out discharge papers for the 1000 draftees at this post, you can all be home for Christmas.

We were all ready to go home a fortnight before Christmas. When the troop train carrying the discharged soldiers stopped for an hour in Los Angeles, I ran to a phone booth and phoned my sister still living and teaching at Pacific Union College. I told her over the phone of my bout with the flu and that remembering the torturous fomentation treatments she had given me so many years ago had saved my life.

I knew she was crying and shedding tears of joy when in a trembling voice she said, "Brother, you omitted the most important Person of all in your recovery from imminent death. You should have said that a loving heavenly Father saved your life." Then she added, "I have a conviction that God saved your life in order that you may do a great work for Him. Please don't fail Him."

My position as an editor of *Signs* at Pacific Press was still open to me. I returned to Mountain View and settled into my editorial job again. In 1922 my sister Alma decided to end her thirty-year teaching career, and I persuaded her to come to Mountain View and live near me and my bride, Eleanor Chapman Baker. We found a place for her to live just across the road from us. The little house still stands on Palo Alto Avenue, just three blocks from Pacific Press.

"Honor Thy Father"

Shortly after moving to Mountain View my sister Alma received an envelope addressed to her bearing in the upper left-hand corner the return address United States Veterans Home, Sawtelle, California.

Alma quickly tore open the envelope and found a short handwritten letter:

"Dear Alma,

I have been very sick for months, so I have come to the Veterans Home in Sawtelle to see if the doctors here can do anything to save my life. They told me this morning they are going to operate on me a few days from now. I have told the hospital here to let you know if I don't make it. They told me I will be buried in the big veterans' cemetery here if I don't survive a major operation.

Your father, Lon Baker."

With tears streaming down her cheeks and with the letter in her hand Alma ran across the road to the house where Eleanor, my wife, and I lived.

"Father is terribly sick at Sawtelle Veterans Home in West Los Angeles," she said, thrusting the letter into my hands. "I must take the next train to Los Angeles and go to him."

She felt she could not put off going even until the next day. We took her to the train station that morning, and she boarded a train for Los Angeles.

When Alma returned, she told my wife and me all about the trip. At the reception desk of the home she inquired about Father. She learned he was seriously ill. The doctors would do a suprapubic prostatectomy on him—just as soon as he recovered somewhat from his long train ride from Colorado.

When she went to the hospital ward and found him on a cot in a twenty-four-bed ward, they both burst into tears, she said.

Father had been so overcome by his eldest daughter's appearance that for some time he sobbed and held both her hands in his. Then he said, "I never expected that you would come down here even for my funeral after all my meanness to your mother."

Alma's reply was typical of her Christian character, "Father, say no more of the days and years now long gone." Then she assured him she would be right back. There were some things that had to be attended to immediately.

"Do you know what I did, Brother?" she asked as a smile suffused her whole face.

"No, Alma, what did you do? I can't imagine you finding your way around the huge metropolis."

"I went to the White Memorial Hospital across town to see my friend Dr. George Thomason. He's a noted Adventist surgeon, you know. I wanted him to do the surgery on our father. When I found Dr. Thomason and told him the story, he said, 'Sister McKibbin, I'll order an ambulance to bring your father here immediately. I'll call the administrator at the Veterans Home to release your father to my care.' "

"What about expenses?" my wife Eleanor asked. "At the Sawtelle Home everything would be free."

"I thought of that," my sister answered. "I thought I could pay for the operation over a period of time; but Dr. Thomason said, 'My dear Sister Alma, there will be no surgical fee and no hospital charge for the father of Mrs. McKibbin. Dr. Percy Magan and I, as well as others here at the White, know full well of the many

Alonzo L. Baker, Sr.

years of distinguished service you have given the denomination. Your years of service have paid in full for
our care of your father.' ''

Alma paused, then added, her voice full of awe, "Can
you imagine that?"

"Father came by ambulance to the White Memorial
Hospital. On the morning of the operation, as was the
custom there, the surgeon bowed his head and prayed.

" 'Almighty Father, I ask that You guide my hand
and my scalpel as I operate on this dear man, Alonzo
Baker. He served his country well in war time and has
over many years been highly respected by his friends
and neighbors as a man of honesty and integrity. I ask
You, our heavenly Father, that You restore Mr. Baker
to good health once more. Amen.' ''

Our father seemed very much impressed with the
prayer of the surgeon. He always delighted in letting
people know about the doctor who had prayed before
he began the surgery.

When Father had recuperated enough and could be moved, Alma brought him home with her to her little house in Mountain View. She gave him the choice front bedroom. She did not want a cent for caring for him, but he insisted he sign over his monthly $75 veteran's check to her.

No more did he rant and rave at the people he had once referred to as "crazy Advents." Now he bowed his head at the table while Alma asked the blessing. He sat quietly and listened during family worship each morning. He had always been very critical and sneering of "Advent grass-eaters," as he called those who did not use flesh foods. Back in Colorado before our family split up, Father demanded Mother to serve huge platters of bacon and eggs each morning. He also wanted many cups of strong black coffee, plus a plateful of hot baking-powder biscuits loaded with butter. He also loved candy and ate it by the sackful.

Now at my sister Alma's home he had either hot oatmeal or granola with whole wheat toast and a glass of milk for breakfast. Around noon Sister served tomato or vegetable soup, a baked potato with gravy, a green vegetable, and either fruit or rice pudding for dessert. Supper, the lightest meal of all, usually consisted of a large glass of warm milk for my sister, but she served Father bread and butter, some fruit, and all the buttermilk he wanted.

On that "Advent diet" our father lived seven years, reduced his weight, and lost his hitherto far-too-large beltline. He had never in his life used tobacco nor any variety of liquor; therefore this was no problem to him. Father seemed to have mellowed a great deal, and he showed his appreciation for my sister's concern for him through the years and now for her tender care.

When friends came to call at my sister's home and she introduced Father to them, he soon began greeting them as Sister ____ or Brother ____. On occasion he attended Sabbath services with my sister Alma in the large Mountain View Church.

Father never formally accepted religion, yet in the last seven years of his life he never voiced the slightest criticism of Adventism or of anybody or anything relating to religion. To all the many friends he made in Mountain View, he often boasted about "My most wonderful daughter, Almee, the best I ever had." He proudly told that she had taught in Advent colleges and had written many textbooks. He would go on to extol her virtues by telling how she had arranged for him to go to an Advent hospital in Los Angeles, where an Advent doctor saved his life. His conversation about his wonderful daughter, whom he called Almee, always ended something like this: "I used to hate Advents like rat poison; but now I think they are great, particularly my daughter Almee, and that Advent doctor in Los Angeles who saved my life."

Seven years after coming to my sister's home, Father passed away. He had only a short illness, went unconscious, and died at midnight. My sister and I stood by his bed praying for him and asking that God's will be done. The doctor who signed the death certificate gave diabetes as the cause of death. In the years previous to his coming to Mountain View he had had too much fatty food, too much cholestrol, too many sweets. But his life had been prolonged those seven years by loving care and nourishing foods. And Father had had the opportunity to see Seventh-day Adventism in action and in all its beauty.

We buried our father in the Alta Mesa cemetery near Mountain View. Since he was a veteran, we gave him a full military funeral. As my wife, Eleanor, and I drove away from the cemetery with my sister Alma in the car with us, I said, "Sister, you surely did your Christian duty when you hurried to Los Angeles to arrange for Father's surgery at the White Memorial Hospital and then brought him home to spend the rest of his life with you in your home. And to think you forgot and forgave him his shameful treatment of our mother."

She replied in a soft, humble voice, "Brother, I was

only obeying the fifth commandment of God's law and Christ's exhortation to 'love one another.' Now I pray that God will raise our father to life in the first resurrection so that he may join us in an eternal life in the new earth.''

There was a smile on her lips as she spoke. That was my sister Alma, always thinking of others and what she could do to help them.

A Growing Experience

Three doors down the street from Alma McKibbin's home lived Harland Johnston and his wife. They had recently come to Mountain View to take charge of the Mountain View Academy. He had never met my sister Alma, but he had become well acquainted with her work as an educator and had used the Bible textbooks she had authored. When he learned that she had given up teaching and had moved almost next door to him, he called upon her one day. In their conversation Professor Johnston told her that he had recently come to Mountain View to head the school and that he had found most of his teachers were young and inexperienced. Then coming right to the point he said, "I want you to join my faculty. You are just what Mountain View Academy needs right now. Will you do it?"

My sister drew back. "Oh, Professor Johnston," she said, "I am happy and flattered by your invitation, but I am fearful that my health—never too good—will not allow me to join your faculty."

Harland Johnston did not accept my sister's negative answer. By the time the school year began, he had persuaded her to be on his faculty. She taught Old and New Testament history classes and denominational history for three years at the academy.

One of Alma's students at the academy, Madge Haines, was the daughter of the man who had been the printing instructor at Healdsburg College years before and who had helped Alma in the production of the shoestring textbook, the first Bible textbooks produced for the denomination. Madge Haines herself became a teacher and spent thirty years in that profession. She also authored a number of books.

"Mrs. McKibbin," Madge often said, "had the rare gift of personalizing all Bible characters to make them come alive. For her they stepped out of the book of Genesis, out of the book of Daniel, out of the book of Luke, out of the book of Acts and came right into our classroom. Moses leading the children of Israel out of Egypt; crossing over on the bottom of the Red Sea; climbing the rocky, rugged Mount Sinai to talk with God; his oration on Mount Nebo—all these were so graphically described by Mrs. McKibbin, who so stimulated our imaginations with her word pictures that at the end of the class period we felt these Old Testament heroes had actually been in the classroom that day.

"Even more graphic were her presentations of New Testament characters. Peter, who denied his Lord, yet was first to enter Joseph's empty tomb on the resurrection morning. Paul the apostle, who spent the first half of his life running down and persecuting Christians. Yes, that same Paul became a defender of the faith. The same Paul who languished in the dark, dank, stench-filled dungeon in Rome's Mamertine prison wrote some of the greatest books of the New Testament.

"Probably Mrs. McKibbin was at her best when she told of the thirty-three earthly years of the life of Jesus—born in a manger, threatened by Herod, forsaken by those He had called as special friends, agonizing in Gethsemane, dying upon the cross, but being resurrected and now sitting at the right hand of the Father. We loved every moment of those classes." Those were the words of one of her students.

During the time she taught in Mountain View Academy, I was ordained to the gospel ministry at a camp meeting held near Oakland. Francis D. Nichol, also one of the *Signs* editors at the Press, was ordained at the same time.

My sister Alma could hardly conceal her pride and joy in my ordination to the gospel ministry. "A loving God gave you to me twenty-four years ago," she said. "You took the place of my own baby boy, Lorin, who lived but eleven months. Now I am sure He has a special place for you in the finishing of the work so we can go home and meet my baby boy and my dear husband again."

In the autumn of 1923, after my ordination, the book committee of the Pacific Press asked me to write a book which would be on the events of the twentieth century portending the second coming of Jesus. Two volumes had been published before: *Our Day in the Light of Prophecy,* by W. A. Spicer, published at the Review and Herald; the other volume published by Pacific Press, authored by editor in chief A. O. Tait, entitled *Heralds of the Morning.* These two volumes the colporteurs had sold with good success. However, the brethren felt the time had come to put out a new book for colporteur sales.

To write a book the type of which would have a definite value to the church and for colporteur sales, I felt the need to do a great deal of research before I began my writing. The Press agreed to allow me the time and to pay my expenses to travel to London, England, where I would study and do research in the British Museum Library, as well as do some traveling and research on the Continent and in the Middle East, if I would forfeit my right to the royalties on the book when it would be published. Such an agreement was worked out.

"The minute you get home, Brother," my sister Alma said when she learned of my plans, "you must come across the road to my house and let me ask you a million questions about the places you saw. I'll take down my large map of Palestine and the Middle East, and you'll have to show me every place that you went."

And that is just what I did when I returned to Mountain View six months later. Alma interrogated and cross-examined me, and her eyes would light up as we traced the journey from place to place on her map.

Her detailed knowledge amazed me. "How in the world did you ever learn all this? You know more about geography and the people of all this area than I do, and only a few weeks ago I saw it with my own eyes."

She smiled. "In old Healdsburg College years and years ago I had R. S. Owen as my teacher in both Old and New Testament history. With the aid of detailed maps and extensive reading and study he took us all over the Bible lands from Ur of the Chaldees and Babylon on the east to Rome on the west. He expected letter-perfect examinations and term papers. It was he who evoked in me a fascination for biblical geography. Then, too, in writing more than a dozen Bible textbooks for Adventist schools and colleges I read and reread many times such books as *Prophets and Kings, Patriarchs and Prophets, Christ's Object Lessons, The Acts of the Apostles,* and *The Desire of Ages.* I did all my reading with a map at hand. But, Brother," she went on, "your description of all the places you have recently visited in person makes it all so much more vivid and real." Her eyes sparkled, and she smiled as she looked up at me. "I am so happy that you, my own brother, have seen with your own eyes what I have seen only in imagination."

The following year, 1925, the book, a 400-page volume entitled *The Hope of the World* was published. It had a large colporteur sale both in Canada and the United States and was translated into several foreign languages. My sister Alma expressed her delight with me in being a well-published author. The material in the book, however, gave her much satisfaction, and she can be credited for having guided and taught me through the years.

Prior to the publication of the book, John T. Scopes, a young high school teacher in Dayton, Tennessee, had been indicted by a Tennessee court because he had dared to teach evolution in his classroom after the Tennessee legislature had declared unlawful the teaching of any doctrine denying the creation of man as taught by the Bible.

A trial date was set for July 1925. Clarence Darrow, a noted criminal defense lawyer, had been employed by Scopes as his defender. The state named William Jennings Bryan to head the prosecution.

Bryan had been a leading orator in America for many years; now his popularity increased even more, and he was inundated with requests from all over the nation for him to lecture.

Francis Nichol and I decided to ask the Pacific Press to invite Bryan to come to Mountain View and deliver his current lecture on the creation versus evolution theory.

The board of directors of the Pacific Press agreed, and William Jennings Bryan received and accepted an invitation to come to Mountain View on a date acceptable to both parties.

Nichol and I met him in San Francisco and brought him to Mountain View on the day set. The Press had planned a special luncheon in honor of the man that day. The members of the city council, the mayor, pastors of all the churches in town, editor of the local newspaper, principals of the town's high school and two grammar schools—as well as Pacific Press board of directors and heads of departments—were all invited to attend the luncheon.

Bryan won his way into the hearts of the assembled group at luncheon with his humor and anecdotes. He spoke of his three-time nomination for the presidency of the United States on the Democratic ticket, remarking, "I always wanted to live rent free in that big house painted white at 1600 Pennsylvania Avenue in Washington, but never quite made it."

It had been arranged that the lecture would be given in the Mountain View high school auditorium. In order to pay the lecture fee, tickets had been sold previously —reserved seat tickets 50 cents each, general admission 25 cents. All seats had been sold out two weeks prior to the time. On arriving at the auditorium we found a capacity crowd.

The audience sat entranced for two hours as Bryan lectured. He extolled Tennessee's lawmakers for outlawing the teaching of evolution in the public schools. He predicted that Clarence Darrow's defense would be a personal bitter attack on Moses and the Bible and upon all "the illiterate and ignoramuses" who put any stock in the Bible at all, which Darrow had said was but a compilation of Jewish folklore.

I had reserved a seat for my sister Alma on the very front row. I kept watching her as Bryan spoke. When he eulogized Moses so truthfully and artfully, I saw my sister's face glow. I knew Moses was her favorite Old Testament character. Hearing this man lecture on the value of the Creation story and the place of Moses in the affairs of man brought great joy to my sister. As usual, her eyes filled with tears of joy. It was a characteristic of Alma that when she was overwhelmed with happiness the tears simply had to flow.

Newspapers near and far featured the story of William Jennings Bryan's visit to Mountain View sponsored by the editors of *Signs of the Times* magazine.

Within hours after the news releases editor in chief A. O. Tait received a phone call from a Dr. Maynard Shipley of San Francisco, an honor graduate from Stanford University and president of the Science League of America. The two men conversed over the phone for a half hour, Dr. Shipley doing most of the talking.

After hanging up the phone Tait called F. D. Nichol and me into his office and told us that the very articulate Dr. Shipley had berated Bryan and any who had any "truck" with him. He had challenged Elder Tait to a debate on "the idiotic creation theory of Moses." Tait paused for a few moments in his conversation with us. Then, tapping his pencil on his desk and frowning slightly, he said, "I want you two men to debate the irate and rather feisty Dr. Shipley."

We agreed, and the board of directors sanctioned the debate. Then Tait called Dr. Shipley and told him the challenge to debate had been accepted. "I will not debate with you," Tait said. "I have assigned that privilege to two of my young assistants."

Shipley asked for a résumé on the two assistants.

"Oh, I don't think they have any résumés," Tait replied.

A pause.

Tait spoke again. "Both of them are honor graduates from Pacific Union College at Angwin, California."

There was a pause.

"Never heard of it?" Tait answered after pausing to listen to Shipley's reply. Then he said, "I want to warn you, Dr. Shipley, that you will have your hands full when you debate with these two sharp young men."

A few days later Nichol and I went to San Francisco to meet Dr. Shipley and to make plans for the debate.

"What were your majors in college?" Dr. Shipley asked, looking from one of us to the other.

"I majored in theology with a minor in history," F. D. Nichol answered.

"And I majored in history with a minor in religion," I answered.

"What? No science?" Shipley almost shouted. "Here I am with a Ph.D. in science from Stanford scheduled to debate with two 'know-nothings' in science."

To which I replied, "Why not let the judges decide whether or not Nichol and I are 'know-nothings'? Let's get on with the plans for our discussion."

We decided that the first night Dr. Shipley would take the affirmative side in the debate that the earth and all life upon it are the results of evolution. Francis Nichol would take the opposition.

The following night the resolution would be That the teaching of evolution should be debarred from tax-supported schools. I would take the affirmative side on this while Dr. Shipley would take the opposition.

After much negotiation three judges and a chairman were settled upon, and they consented to sit as judges at the debate: chairman, Maurice E. Harrison, the dean at the Hastings School of Law, University of California; Honorable Wallace McCamant, judge of the United States Circuit Court of Appeals; Honorable F. H. Kerrigan, judge of the Federal District Court; Honorable D. A. Cashin, associate justice of the Appellate Court of California.

The dates June 13 and 14, 1925, were agreed upon for the debate; and it would be held in the Native Sons Hall on Van Ness Avenue in San Francisco.

When the details of time and place and judges had been taken care of to our mutual satisfaction, Nichol and I began to prepare ourselves for the presentation. We went to professors at both Stanford and the University of California at Berkeley to ask about the newest and most authoritative books presenting the case of Darwin's theory. Then we ordered all the books they listed for us. For weeks we poured over those volumes, making hundreds of notes.

News stories began to appear in all the newspapers for San Francisco, Oakland, Palo Alto, and San Jose. The copy always featured Dr. Shipley, president of the Science League of America. The reference made to Nichol and me was always the same, "Two young associate editors of a Seventh-day Adventist Church magazine published in Mountain View."

The evening of June 13 arrived. Dr. Shipley constantly brought out the thought that "only the anti-intellectuals and those of little or no education still believe in the archaic Bible account of Creation."

Nichol came to the speaker's lecturn carrying an armful of the books we had purchased and spent so many hours perusing, books all commended to us by Stanford and University of California professors. He cited passage after passage from these books in which the authors repeatedly used such phrasing as "It is conjectured that—" "It may be that—" "We don't know for a certainty, but it may be that—"

"My worthy opponent," Dr. Shipley jibed in his rebuttal, "is so lacking in academic accomplishment that he does not understand what he read from the books cited."

The next evening I took the position that since the topic of Creationism versus Darwinian Evolution inevitably involves a religious issue—the denial of the validity of Genesis 1:1 to 3 in the Christian Bible—therefore such teaching in a tax-supported school is in violation of the First Amendment of the Constitution of the United States of America.

Dr. Shipley scoffed at my contention.

When the judges came in with their decision, a silence filled the hall. Dean Harrison, the chairman, stepped up to the lectern. The decision was as follows: "The earth and all life upon it are *not* the result of evolution; and second, the teaching of evolution should *not* be debarred from tax-supported schools."

On both evenings of the debate I had brought my sister Alma to the hall and had arranged for her to have a front seat. When I came off the stage after the judges' decision had been read, my sister stood at the foot of the steps waiting for me. She threw her arms about me and said, "Brother, this is the happiest moment in all the twenty-six years since you took the place of my baby boy, Lorin. In every minute of your presentation tonight defending the Mosaic account of Creation, my one regret was that our mother was not here to see her boy so ably defend the Bible.

I held this dear little woman close to my heart. She had been like a mother to me through the years. Had it not been for her care, her diligent teaching and instructing, reproving and praising me through the years, I might not have become the person I was then and now am.

Toward the Sunset Years

After teaching three years at the academy in Mountain View and taking care of our father so long and so tenderly, my sister Alma deserved a rest. But Sister could never sit by idly and think of her own creature comforts. At first her close friends came to her to talk over their problems and pray with her. Her students came for counseling. And it soon became evident to Eleanor and me, who lived across the road, that sister Alma had little time to herself. Troubled and harrassed people came to her constantly for comfort, sympathy, and hope. Many came with tears in their eyes. A half hour, or even an hour or two later, we saw them coming out of the door, down the steps to the sidewalk, with sister Alma walking beside them holding them by a hand or arm. Her callers always left with hope glowing on their faces and a spring in their step.

A wise person once said, "Let a man make a better mousetrap, and the world will beat a path to his door." My sister never made a mousetrap, but people did beat a path to her door. Comfort, sympathy, and hope— those three things are worth more than ten thousand mousetraps, and those three commodities my sister Alma provided for the people who came to her home at 525 Palo Alto Avenue in Mountain View.

My sister could sympathize with the sick, for she had never had a truly well day since she had been so near death in the spring of 1892, just before her graduation and just before her marriage. Both her husband and their eleven-month-old son died a few short years later.

Her counseling methods came not from a college textbook on The Art of Counseling, written by some graduate student who did a thesis in order to be awarded a Ph.D. Her counseling came out of forty, fifty, sixty years of actual life experiences.

People came with marital problems; parents came who had problems with their wayward and rebellious children; people came whose Christian experience was floundering; people came who had been told by their doctor that theirs was a terminal illness; people came who had recently lost a loved one by death.

My sister Alma had the rare gift of sympathy. Her sympathy consisted not of a superficial type: "Oh, I am so sorry; I wish there was something I could do to help you. I do hope things will soon make a turn for the better."

Rather, Alma encouraged her troubled visitors to tell the full story behind their despair. Then my sister would talk to God in audible prayer asking Him for guidance in advising her deeply troubled friend.

The McKibbin home became a place of refuge for the troubled, the perplexed, and the despairing. Over the years of her retirement Alma McKibbin lifted the spirits, inspired new hopes, gave spiritual rebirth to hundreds and hundreds of men and women.

Another remarkable aspect of my sister Alma's sunset years was her response to the constant demand from Adventist groups everywhere for her to speak publicly of early Adventist history, the primitive days of Adventist education. She was delighted to respond to such requests, even when she was in her mid-nineties. Whether speaking in the Mountain View Church to the large membership there or at the Central California Conference camp meeting, one of the largest camp meetings in North America, my sister Alma spoke clearly and well without script or notes. Her delight was to tell of what God had done in the past for His people and what He would do now and in the future.

One day when my sister was well into her ninetieth year a letter came to my home from Dr. Charles E. Weniger, then teaching in the seminary in Takoma Park, Washington. The letter said that at a recent reunion of one-time Pacific Union College students in and around Takoma Park, the group discussed former teachers at P.U.C. "All in the group agreed," said Dr. Weniger, "that of all the faculty at P.U.C. the one they admired the most was none other than Mrs. McKibbin." He went on to write that each one present had said he wished to see her again. Then he added, "Do you think, Lonnie, that this would be possible?"

Eleanor and I talked over the idea. Of course it would be possible, we agreed. And immediately I purchased a round-trip ticket from San Francisco to Washington, D.C., on a Pan-American nonstop flight, reserving a window seat for a certain date.

When all the arrangements had been made, we told my sister as casually as we could. "Sister, on such and such a date you are flying from San Francisco to Washington, D.C. When you arrive there a few short hours later, you will be met at the airport by Charles and Eunice Weniger, Francis and Rose Nichol, and Lambert Moffitt and his wife. The six of them are a committee set up to entertain you for at least a fortnight. You will see everything worth seeing in Washington and Takoma Park and their environs."

At first she looked at us blankly. Then she burst into a flood of joyous tears. "Next to the New Jerusalem in heaven above, seeing our nation's capital city and our Adventist international headquarters in Takoma Park is the greatest privilege an old lady of my age could possibly have."

Upon returning home she told us, "No head of state visiting Washington, D.C., ever received a more magnificent reception. I was feted and adulated, wined and dined, and toured through both houses of Congress, the

Congressional Library, the White House, Lincoln's magnificent Memorial, the Tomb of the Unknown Soldier, George Washington's Mount Vernon home down the Potomac River, and—and the General Conference headquarters and the Review and Herald Publishing Association, and I met all the important people in both institutions." Her face glowed with happiness as she spoke.

"You enjoyed it all?" I asked.

"Enjoyed it, did you say? Enjoy is too weak a word. I was in rapture every minute of the time. Never until after the great resurrection and I fly to heaven with my loved ones will I be so happy as I have been the past two weeks."

Eleanor and I had moved from Mountain View to Stockton, California, where I taught for a number of years at the University of the Pacific. We often drove back to Mountain View to visit my sister Alma. In the remaining thirteen years of her life she always spoke of the "great travel joy of my life, that trip to Washington, D.C."

When my sister reached ninety-seven years of age, her failing health and ability to look after herself made it necessary for Eleanor and me to put her in a convalescent hospital in Cupertino, operated by Seventh-day Adventists.

In a talk given at the Mountain View Church some time before she went to the convalescent hospital she remarked, "Soon it may be time to say good-night with a smile. Let me testify that it is good to serve God, who has led me all the way. The greatest lesson I have learned is that a cheerful submission to the will of God is the secret of success in a Christian's life. 'He knoweth the way that I take: when He hath tried me, I shall come forth as gold.' Job 23:10."

During the year 1972 after my sister had reached her one hundredth year she received an honorary doctorate conferred upon her by Pacific Union College, where she had taught so many years before. One year later she was

ERIC KREYE

Dr. Alma McKibbin, at age 101, received an honorary doctorate from Dr. Floyd O. Rittenhouse, president of Pacific Union College. Standing beside Dr. Rittenhouse is Mrs. McKibbin's niece, Helen Morris.

Dr. Charles Hirsch, director of education for the Seventh-day Adventist Church, and Dr. Wilbert Schneider, director of education of the Pacific Union Conference, conferred upon Alma McKibbin the denomination's "Medallion of Merit" for her more than seventy-five years of outstanding contribution to Adventist education.

awarded the Adventist Medallion of Merit by Dr. Charles Hirsch, worldwide Seventh-day Adventist director of education, and Dr. Wilbert Schneider, Pacific Union Conference director of education. The award honored my sister Alma for her more than seventy-five years of outstanding contribution to Adventist education. She was but the fifth educator in Adventist history to receive such a high degree. She is credited as being California's first church school teacher, and she authored the first Bible textbooks. These shoestring Bible textbooks, so called because the first copies were held together by shoestrings, were used throughout the United States, Canada, and in many foreign countries. Only two of the original copies are still existent today.

Some time in the night of July 16, 1974, well into her one hundred and third year, my sister died in her sleep. Without premonition or pain she simply ceased breathing. Those who went to wake her in the morning said her face glowed with the peace of God.

I had gone on an overseas study tour, leading twenty-five Americans. This tour was my sixth. We were in Irkutsk, central Siberia. Then we flew to Tokyo. When I arrived at the hotel, the man at the desk said, "Dr. Baker, your wife in California is very anxious to have you call her the minute you check in."

When I reached her by phone, she told me that my sister had passed away. She had tried to reach me in Moscow at the Hotel Rossiya but had had no luck.

"When can you come home?" she asked. "Alma passed away a week ago. We've been trying our best to reach you."

"I'll be home within fifteen hours," I answered. "I'll phone you from the airport giving you the exact time of my arrival in San Francisco."

The time of the funeral had been postponed until my return from overseas. Now we scheduled it to be held in the Mountain View Church, where my sister had been a member for fifty-three years. That Sabbath afternoon, July 28, the church was full. So many had come to bid farewell to one they had learned to love and trust and who had been such a comfort to many of them. The president of the Central California Conference, Elder Earl Amundsen, officiated, assisted by Elders Douglas Marchus and Richard Utt. I, Lonnie Baker, Alma's brother, whom she had loved and cared for as a mother would her own child throughout the years, gave a life sketch and a eulogy to the "most wonderful sister any brother ever had."

Many years before, Alma had requested that when she died she wanted to be buried beside her mother in the Healdsburg cemetery on the lower slope of Mount Fitch. There we finally and lovingly placed her body in the Oakmont Cemetery, not far from the site of the Old

Healdsburg College, that she had loved so much.

One of the members of the Mountain View Church, Richard Anderson, a mortician and manager of a local mortuary, arranged all the details and the services both in Mountain View and in Healdsburg.

At the graveside in Oakmont Cemetery, Elders Ernest Lloyd and Ned Bristow had a part. Elder Ernest Lloyd and his wife, Beulah, had lived next door to my sister Alma all the twenty-five years that Elder Lloyd had been editor of *Our Little Friend*. Also at the graveside service were Bert and Evelyn Anderson from Mountain View, father and mother of Richard Anderson, the mortician. Bert had been one of Alma's students at Pacific Union College. Evelyn had been a student of hers at the Mountain View Academy.

After the graveside ceremony, as we were leaving the cemetery, Evelyn Anderson handed me an envelope tied with a blue ribbon. "I'm sure you will be interested in a letter written by your sister Alma just forty-nine years ago to this day."

I untied the blue ribbon and took out the letter in the envelope. The letter had been written in my sister's beautiful, immaculate handwriting. It was dated Mountain View, July 28, 1925.

"My Dear Evelyn:

I am thinking of you on the morning of your 'happy day,' and wishing for you that all your days will be happy days.

"It has been said, 'All the world loves a lover,' and I suppose that is the reason I feel so happy when I think that this is your wedding day. It seems almost as if I hear the joybells ringing.

"I pray that the new home on our street may not be a house only but a home—a real home where angels shall love to dwell. The world has great need of such homes. I know of no greater mission today than those who know the precious truth that Jesus is coming soon should establish and maintain true Christian homes,—give to the world an example of what a home should be,—'a little heaven here below to go to heaven in,' as someone has said.

"The world is full of homes, and oh so many broken homes! that mankind is losing faith in marriage altogether, or at best it is disparaged in their minds as a failure.

"I pray, dear Evelyn, that you and Bert may make a real home,—one that may help to restore faith in the hearts of men, make them still to believe in God's first plan for man and woman. What greater mission or work could one have than to live a great and holy principle!

"I wish you much joy, contentment, and happiness. May your joys be increased and your griefs diminished because they are shared.

"There is a paradoxical saying that every home to be a happy one must have two bears in it always—bear and forbear. Strange to say these two animals never growl. They seem to be new-earth animals.

"I love you, Evelyn, and shall always be interested in your present and eternal welfare. Your name is not only in my school book of 'Remembrances,' but in my heart also.

"I will take no more of your time on your beautiful wedding day only again to wish you well with all my heart's best love.

"Your former teacher and friend always, Alma E. McKibbin"

Since that July day when I left the graves of Mother and my sister Alma, my supreme desire is some glorious day to have a mansion in heaven on gold-paved Redemption Avenue. Directly across Redemption Avenue in another mansion will live my sister Alma with her son, Lorin, and her husband, Edwin. Living with my Eleanor and me part time will be Mother, Stella Baker, who will also live part time with Alma, Edwin, and Lorin. Mother will alternate between my sister and me every thousand years or so. I hope my father, Alonzo Lafayette Baker, Sr., will be there too.

As I read over and over Isaiah 11:1-9 and Revelation

21 and 22, I look forward to that day when we shall all be caught up together in the clouds and so shall we ever be with the Lord. "God shall wipe away all tears from their eyes; and there shall be no more death . . . : for the former things are passed away." Revelation 21:4.

The God of my sister Alma, and mine and yours, is a God of reality, not of fantasy! He says, "Behold, I come quickly: blessed is he that keepeth the sayings of the prophecy of this book."

And with all those people like my sister Alma, the cry still goes up to God, "Even so, come, Lord Jesus."

Berniece P. Blake completed reading this beautifully written boo February 16, 1982. I found it very interesting!

I read this wonderful book again May 26-28, 1987 and Enjoyed it as much as I de the first time!

I completed reading out to Becky, Friedric, & Erwin Marc 2, 1989 We enjoyed it very mu
BOB

Rebecca Knolls Aug 9 '200 finished reading this lovely book

Alma McKibbin Celebrates 100th Birthday Soon

On Friday, November 26, Mrs. Alma E. McKibbin, pioneer Adventist educator and textbook author, will celebrate her 100th birthday. All of Mrs. McKibbin's teaching career has been in California since the day in 1889 when she arrived at Healdsburg College from Colorado. She was graduated from that school 81 years ago when Healdsburg was the only Adventist college in existence with the exception of Battle Creek.

Not long after graduation, Mrs. McKibbin started the first church school in southern California in the San Pasqual Valley. Later she was the first teacher in the Santa Ana church school.